D1528594

LEADING
WOMEN

Aung San Suu Kyi

RUTH BJORKLUND

Cavendish
Square

New York

Published in 2014 by Cavendish Square Publishing, LLC
303 Park Avenue South, Suite 1247, New York, NY 10010

Copyright © 2014 by Cavendish Square Publishing, LLC

First Edition

Library of Congress Cataloging-in-Publication Data
Bjorklund, Ruth.
Aung San Suu Kyi / Ruth Bjorklund.
p. cm. — (Leading women)
Includes bibliographical references and index.
Summary: "Presents the biography of Aung San Suu Kyi against the backdrop of her political, historical, and cultural environment"—Provided by publisher.
ISBN 978-0-7614-4957-7 (hardcover) ISBN 978-1-62712-115-6 (paperback)
ISBN 978-1-60870-714-0 (ebook)
1. Aung San Suu Kyi. 2. Women political activists—Burma—Biography—Juvenile literature. 3. Women, Burmese—Biography—Juvenile literature. 4. Burma—Politics and government—Juvenile literature. I. Title. II. Series.
HQ1735.7.Z75A853 2012
959.105092—dc22
[B]
Editor: Deborah Grahame-Smith   Series Designer: Nancy Sabato   Art Director: Anahid Hamparian
Photo research by Connie Gardner

Printed in the United States of America

CONTENTS

Aung San Suu Kyi greets her supporters, November 2010.

A Worker for Democracy

AUNG SAN SUU KYI, THE FEARLESS LEADER of Burma's pro-democracy movement, has battled for free elections and basic human rights for the Burmese people for more than three decades. Her efforts angered the powerful ruling military elite that sought to silence her with arrest and intimidation. As a consequence, Aung San Suu Kyi has spent more than fifteen out of the last twenty-one years under some form of detention. From behind the guarded walls of her home, Aung San Suu Kyi remained a powerful voice urging the Burmese to stay faithful to their democratic principles.

On November 7, 2010, Burma held its first national elections since 1989. While the military elite retained control of the government, days later, on November 13, the officials released Aung San Suu Kyi from her latest detention. As she met with the adoring throngs of Burmese who waited to greet her outside of her gates, she promised to be a "worker for democracy." At sixty-five years of age her bravery and resolve has stayed strong. She knows that there are risks in her role as a spokesperson for democracy but says,

My attitude is, do as much as I can while I'm free. And if I'm arrested I'll still do as much as I can.

CHAPTER ONE

Leading Lady

O N THE STEPS OF THE TOWERING, gold-covered Shwedagon Pagoda in Rangoon, Burma, before hundreds of thousands of fellow citizens, a poised young woman dressed in a flowered sarong and a simple pair of sandals raised her voice and inspired a nation. Behind her, a banner displayed the image of her father, the slain Burmese general Aung San. It was August 26, 1988. This crowd had revered the man on the banner, the hero they called *Bogyoke* (General). However, they did not know much about the elegant, foreign-educated woman standing before them.

The general's daughter, Aung San Suu Kyi (pronounced Aoun [as in "sound"] Sahn Sue Chee), believed it was her political duty to return to her homeland. She felt compelled to urge Burma's military government to end its violent attacks on citizens and to allow the people to elect their leaders democratically. On that day in August, she declared,

I believe that all the people who have assembled here have without exception come with the unshakable desire to strive for and win a multi-party democratic system.

Aung San Suu Kyi stands before a poster
honoring her late father, General Aung San.

From that moment on, the daughter of Burma's most beloved military hero became the new hope for a long-persecuted nation. The people have bestowed on her an honorific title as well: the Lady.

Aung San Suu Kyi often said,

When I honor my father, I honor all those who stand for political integrity in Burma.

General Aung San had devoted his life to the independence of the Burmese people. Born in central Burma on February 13, 1915, Aung San followed in his family's footsteps by joining the resistance movement seeking to free Burma from British colonial rule. In his youth, Aung San studied at a Buddhist monastery, where he learned self-discipline and moral responsibility. Students in Burmese monastery schools came from a variety of ethnic and social backgrounds. All students—from members of the Burmese royalty to villagers from a tribal minority—were considered equal.

For high school, Aung San attended the Yenangyaung National School. The national schools of Burma had been established in 1920 as a reaction to a British law, the Rangoon University Act, which stated that only students from prominent, wealthy families could attend the country's universities. Most students at the national schools were fiercely dedicated to the cause of Burmese independence. At Yenangyaung, Aung San immersed himself in the study of famous political figures, honed his debating skills, and developed his own style of political oratory.

After completing school with the highest of honors, Aung San entered Rangoon University. He was elected to the students' union and became editor of the students' union magazine, *Oway*. He also wrote articles for leading Burmese magazines. Aung San became more and more involved in student resistance to British rule. In 1935, *Oway* published an article entitled "Hell Hound at Large." It described a recent event in which a Rangoon University student accused a white British professor of indecent conduct. The administrators of the university took the side of the professor and expelled the student. Once *Oway*'s exposé appeared, the administrators demanded that Aung San release the name of the article's author. Aung San refused, and he, too, was expelled. Nearly one-third of Rangoon University's two thousand students gathered in protest at the steps of the Shwedagon Pagoda. They called for a boycott of classes and exams.

People throughout Rangoon admired the students for their actions against the British. They especially admired Aung San for his loyalty to the writer of the article. The protest and boycott were successful. The university administrators asked the faculty members involved in the incident to resign. They also reinstated the students who had been expelled. And as a result of Aung San's levelheaded leadership, the governor selected the young leader as the sole student representative to the Rangoon University Act Amendment Committee, which had been created to correct injustice in the university's policies.

THE THAKIN

After receiving his bachelor of arts degree in 1937, Aung San planned to attend law school. The political landscape in Burma was changing rapidly, however. Instead of following his original plan, Aung San sent his mother a letter saying that he planned to enter politics.

In 1937, one of the hot issues in British-controlled Burma was the Government of Burma Act. This act was an attempt to grant Burma a small measure of self-government. For many Burmese, however, it was an unsatisfactory compromise. Although the act mandated a native Burmese prime minister and a native cabinet, the British government generally treated the prime minister as a puppet. The parliament and other government offices were also very much slanted in favor of the British. The new law established 132 seats in the lower house of the Burmese Parliament, but 40 of the seats were reserved for special interest groups favorable to the British, such as industrialists, wealthy citizens, and Chinese and Indian businesspeople. The British governor of Burma would retain total veto power over any legislation. Taxing authority, foreign relations, and military departments were to remain under British control.

Many Burmese dissidents intensely disputed the Government of Burma Act. Among them was a group called *Dohbama Asi-ayone* (We-Burmese Organization). Aung San joined the group and became one of its leaders. Members of the group gave the title *thakin*, meaning "master," to their most strident peers. In the general elections of 1937, only two members of the Dohbama Asi-ayone party won a seat in the Burmese Parliament. This outcome did not appease Thakin Aung San.

According to the Burmese calendar, 1938 was the start of a new century, Year 1300. Yet the Burmese would actually remember 1938 as the Year of the Revolution. In August, many disturbances erupted at the same time. Oil field workers, who were angry about unsafe conditions and low wages, staged a protest march to Rangoon. At the same time, 20,000 agricultural workers were at odds with moneylenders and corrupt landlords. They, too, decided to march to Rangoon. University students, hearing of the workers' rage, also planned to march to Rangoon to show their support. The police set up roadblocks and forced the marchers away. But the protesters did not stay away for long. In December, students gathered at a nonviolent rally outside a government building in Rangoon. The police moved in with swinging batons, and one student protester was beaten to death. In the ensuing months, more protesters participated in rallies, walkouts, and other forms of resistance.

Even monks and high school students showed their disapproval of British rule. At a student rally near a pagoda in the city of Mandalay, police tried to break up the crowd with guns. In the end, they wounded many protesters and killed seven monks, nine students, and one child. This tragedy was a turning point for Aung San and his fellow dissidents.

Inside the Dohbama Asi-ayone there was an intense—and ultimately destructive—political rivalry. Forced to choose his allegiance, Aung San gave his loyalty to the majority faction, which was led by a former monk. The faction's leader, in turn, appointed Aung San as general secretary of the organization. Aung San concentrated all his efforts on supporting the people in their resistance to the British.

From within the organization, Aung San coordinated demonstrations and protest rallies, and he helped provide food and shelter for striking workers and marchers. In January 1939, as tensions grew and the police became more aggressive, members of the Dohbama Asi-ayone decided it was time to use force. The organization established a protest camp outside the Shwedagon Pagoda, where thakins, monks, students, and other dissidents could discuss their plans. But the police broke up the gatherings and arrested several participants, including Aung San. They threatened him with the death penalty as punishment for treason, but ultimately they released him fifteen days later without explanation.

On September 3, 1939, Great Britain declared war on Germany in what became World War II. Aung San saw this as an opportunity to drive the British out of Burma. But the British established an emergency law called the Defense of Burma Act, which required the Burmese to ally themselves with Britain. The act gave Britain the right to detain any Burmese citizen for any reason and without a warrant. Thakins were frequent targets of the new law.

Aung San declared,

We cannot contemplate for one moment the question of participation in the present imperialist war for the freedom of another country so long as we are not allowed freedom of action.

He left to seek the counsel and advice of the Indian leaders Mahatma Gandhi and Jawaharlal Nehru. Ready to campaign for independence, he returned to Burma and helped to found the Freedom Bloc party, for which he served as general secretary. During this period, Aung San and his followers studied the socialist and communist beliefs of Mao Tse-tung, Chiang Kai-shek, and Karl Marx.

Aung San believed the Japanese might help drive the British out of Burma. Thirty Burmese soldiers, known as the Thirty Comrades, went to Japan for military training. Aung San Suu Kyi later called this event

the birth of Burma's armed forces.

In July 1942, Aung San became commander in chief of the Burma Defense Army, and was stationed in the jungles of the hill country. He contracted malaria and was hosptialized in Rangoon, where he met a nurse named Khin Kyi (pronounced Kin Chee).

KHIN KYI

Khin Kyi was the eighth of ten children. An ethnic Burman, she attended primary school in Myaungmya, a city with a large ethnic Karen population. She went on to boarding school and then attended the Morton Lane Teacher Training College in Moulmein, an important British colonial center. Khin Kyi returned to Myaungmya to teach. But Khin Kyi wanted to see more of the world than her childhood home, so she decided to attend nursing school. Khin Kyi's mother strongly objected to this career change. Upper-class Burmans regarded the teaching occupation highly but viewed nursing as inappropriate for promising young people. Khin Kyi's mother felt that if her daughter was determined to study medicine, she should become a doctor and not a nurse. Yet Khin Kyi ultimately had her way and left home to study nursing in Rangoon.

Khin Kyi took an internship as a nurse at the Rangoon General Hospital. In short order, she stood out among her peers as exceptionally determined, thorough, and astute. She also joined the Women's

Freedom League, an organization established to achieve women's rights and to promote Burmese patriotism.

By the time Khin Kyi began her nursing career, the war dominated most of Burma. The Japanese had invaded, and the British had abandoned most efforts to maintain authority. The British Army was made up of mostly Indian soldiers, who were exhausted and weakened from defending the colony. Many soldiers had developed malaria from fighting in the Burmese jungles. Many more were seriously wounded due to repeated Japanese bombings of Rangoon.

Japanese soldiers prepare to cross the border into Burma as part of their World War II campaign to defeat the British and oust them from the country.

The Americans and the British ordered foreigners to leave, and most Burmese also fled the city. The Indian soldiers who were physically able left their posts and returned home. But many soldiers were too sick or disabled to join the exodus. The Rangoon General Hospital's director decided that the most humane action was to send the remaining soldiers to Calcutta, India, in a hospital ship. Few medical personnel remained at the hospital in Rangoon, and fewer still were willing to risk the journey. But Khin Kyi volunteered to accompany the soldiers home, and when she was ready to return she boarded the last ship allowed to leave India. Behind her, the Japanese slammed shut the borders and closed Burmese shipping lanes to foreign vessels.

Due to her highly regarded status at the Rangoon General Hospital, Khin Kyi was assigned to care for its highest-profile patient, General Aung San. The Bogyoke was suffering from malaria and overall exhaustion. Accustomed to being in command, Aung San had difficulty allowing others to care for him and to make decisions on his behalf. As a patient, he was argumentative and uncooperative. Khin Kyi handled her obstreperous charge with firmness and grace. Against his own advice that a soldier should avoid becoming romantically involved, the Bogyoke fell in love and married his nurse.

THE WAR'S END

The Japanese, now in power, promoted Aung San to war minister and declared that Burma would soon become independent. Aung San wanted to unify all the people of Burma, and he attempted to get along with the Japanese government. However, Aung San soon realized that the Japanese were not upholding their promises and had no intention of relinquishing control over Burma. In response, he helped found the Anti-Fascist People's Freedom League (AFPFL) to resist Japanese imperialism.

The Burmese army joined forces with the United States, Britain, and their allies to overcome the Japanese. The Japanese surrendered August 15, 1945. In a speech, the Bogyoke urged his comrades to work toward true independence: "Now the war is over, and we have also achieved a complete national solidarity mobilized behind the Anti-Fascist People's Freedom League. All are now united—united, I say, to march together to our common goal of freedom."

Aung San believed his people would unify and prosper as an independent nation. Before an audience of the AFPFL Supreme Council in 1946, he enjoined party members with these words:

WORK, WORK, WORK, ACTION, ACTION, ACTION, SELF-RELIANCE, SELF-RELIANCE, SELF-RELIANCE. This is the stern, simple golden rule of timeless truth for any success that man makes. And there is no other rule which comes first before it.

In 1947, in an effort to strengthen ties between ethnic groups and the central government, Aung San and other government leaders signed the Panglong (pronounced Pin-loun with an "ou" sound as in "ouch") Agreement with the British creating the Federal Union of Burma and granting some political autonomy to local ethnic governments.

After Aung San was elected president of the AFPFL, his party won 196 of 202 seats in the Burmese Parliament. Convinced his

Children celebrate the Allies victory on August 9, 1945, the day the second atomic bomb was dropped on Japan, leading to the Japanese surrender.

dreams of independence for Burma were coming to fruition, Aung San urged his comrades to join in his demands to the British:

> **We want to have elections to . . . form a Constituent Assembly free from any foreign control, to frame a constitution for a free, independent Burma. These are our clear, simple basic demands. Can the people of Burma realize these basic demands? Yes, I think we can.**

In 1947, Aung San was the delegate sent to London to sign the Aung San–Attlee Agreement, which would grant Burma independence in 1948.

THE LADY'S MOTHER

Burmese freedom *was* reliant on the unity and common purpose of the people. Daw Khin Kyi helped Aung San to achieve this common purpose in countless ways. (*Daw* is Burmese for "madam" or, literally, "auntie.") Born a Burman, Khin Kyi's mother was a devout Buddhist. But her father had many Muslim and Christian friends and employees, and he eventually became a Baptist. Daw Khin Kyi's father urged her to practice the faith of her choice and to believe that all people and tribes of Burma were equals.

Daw Khin Kyi's understanding of other religions and ethnic cultures within Burma was an enormous asset to Aung San. Daw Khin Kyi would often accompany the Bogyoke as he visited tribal villages in the mountains and jungles. When visitors came to her home, Daw Khin Kyi was a gracious hostess who put everyone at ease. This helped offset Aung San's sometimes gruff demeanor. During the fierce battles and bombings in Rangoon, Daw Khin Kyi was steady by Aung San's side. At one point in the war, when the general was on a particularly dangerous mission, it was necessary for Daw Khin Kyi to go into hiding. Once, she smuggled her children into a remote area along the Irrawaddy River. She either avoided or outsmarted the Japanese patrols.

The general's family was precious to him. He longed for a day when the struggle to free his nation from imperialism ceased to be necessary. His daughter, Aung San Suu Kyi, commented sadly,

> During the last months of his life, he often spoke wistfully of the time he could leave his grinding duties and live quietly with his family. All good things were to come with Independence but it came six months too late for him.

On July 19, 1947, when Aung San Suu Kyi was only two years old, General Aung San, along with his brother, U Ba Win, and five other executive councilors of the government, were gunned down by assassins hired by a former prime minister and political rival, U Saw.

As a widow, Daw Khin Kyi embarked on a twenty-year career in public service. Her first position was that of director of the National Women's and Children's Welfare Board. In 1953, she was appointed chairwoman of the Social Planning Commission and helped

Aung San Suu Kyi, at age two, sits on her father's lap shortly before he was assassinated.

organize the women's wing of the National Union party. In 1960, she became the first woman to be appointed as an ambassador by the Burmese government. She took her post in India and served her country well for seven years.

Upon returning to Burma, Daw Khin Kyi was not pleased with the authoritarian government and lack of progress that she found there. She continued to work on quality-of-life issues for the Burmese. Acting as the Burmese delegate to the World Health Organization, she represented her country in international relations. The U.S. government dubbed Daw Khin Kyi the Mother of Burma, and she received accolades and awards from many other nations.

After years of service to Burma and its people, Daw Khin Kyi withdrew from public life. But she did not do so without first having set an example for her daughter. And so, in Beijing during the 1995 United Nations World Conference on Women, her daughter Aung San Suu Kyi, a political prisoner, said in a videotaped speech,

"It is not the prerogative of men alone to bring light to this world: women with their capacity for compassion and self-sacrifice, their courage and perseverance, have done much to dissipate the darkness of intolerance and hate, suffering and despair."

CHAPTER TWO

The Painful History of the Golden Land

B URMA, WHICH THE MILITARY GOVERNMENT renamed as the Union of Myanmar in 1989, is one of the most beautiful and bountiful countries in the world. But also has had its share of tragedy, however. Home to a diverse, multiethnic population of about 48 million, Burma's ancient cultural traditions are still alive. Its people refer to their nation as the Golden Land. Yet its splendor has withered under what many cite as one of the world's most repressive governments.

The fortieth-largest country in the world, Burma has a geographic abundance and a wealth of natural resources. The land is a wide expanse of plains and valleys surrounded by towering mountains and rain forest. Many lakes and rivers, including Inya Lake and the Irrawaddy River, provide both nourishment and hydropower. The Irrawaddy River, at 1,350 miles (2,170 kilometers) long, is the country's major waterway. It originates in the north, carves deep canyons through the Himalayas, spills into lowlands, and widens into one of the world's largest deltas before emptying into the Bay of Bengal. The river creates unparalleled fertile farmland. Burma was once called the rice bowl of Asia, producing and exporting more rice than any other Asian country, until the military drove out the farmers and confiscated their holdings.

The Golden Land's natural resources are state controlled and the exporting of rubies, pearls, jade, and sapphires fills government coffers as does trading in natural gas, oil, and precious

A view across the Irrawaddy River valley toward the ancient capital city of Bagan, Manadalay, historic site of Buddhist monuments, many dating back to the tenth century CE.

metals. Teak, an exotic hardwood once logged by elephants, continues to be harvested from Burma's endangered rain forests.

Burma's population is composed of more than a hundred racial and ethnic groups, including the Mon, Burman, Kachin, Chin, Shan, Rakhine (Arakanese), Rohingya, Wa, and Karen. Traditionally, the groups lived in separate regions controlled by tribal rulers and other local governors. Today, Burma is still divided into ethnic states and divisions, but the military's central government rules them all.

In the western part of the country, Rakhine State borders the Bay of Bengal, which is part of the Indian Ocean. Farther north lie Chin State and Kachin State. These regions form a mountainous border with India. Along this border, which includes the Himalayas, the Naga Hills, and the Chin Hills, some of the peaks rise to more than 12,000 feet (3,650 meters). The northern Kachin State and the western Shan State border southwestern China. The Shan State also borders Laos. Slicing through these regions is the Mekong River. Bordering Thailand on the southeast are the Karen State, the Karenni State, and a long sliver of land called the Tanintharyi Region. Between the Tanintharyi Region and the Andaman Sea is the Mon State. Most of Burma's people live in the central broad valleys, in the Rangoon, Mandalay, Magwe, Pegu, and Irrawaddy divisions.

With all its ethnic groups, Burma is one of the most culturally diverse countries in the world. Some of the groups share customs in clothing, food, religion, and language, while others have unique practices. The largest ethnic group is the Burman. More than 65 percent of all Burmese speak only the Burman language. *Burmese* is the term used to describe a citizen of Burma, while *Burman* is used to describe a member of the Burman ethnic group. Burmans follow rich cultural traditions in music, dance, theater. They tend to be well educated, particularly in the fields of philosophy, government, art, and medicine. The Burmans are devout Buddhists, and both men and women generally wear traditional garb—sarongs, known as *longyis*.

More than 2 million Karens make up Burma's second-largest ethnic group, which is closely related to Thais. They live in the hill country, which is covered in forest and jungle. Karens are farmers, growing cash crops such as rice and corn. Their religion is a mixture of Buddhism, animism, and Christianity, the latter introduced by Baptist missionaries in the nineteenth century. Karens are ferociously nationalistic, due to abuse by the Burmese kings and later by the British. During World War II, they fought with the British against the Japanese invasion. At the end of the war, however, the

Girls of the Kayan tribe, a subgroup of the Karen tribe, are known for their "long neck" jewelry—brass rings that encircle their necks.

British made promises they never kept. Since then the Karens have maintained a resistance army, with the goal of becoming independent of any form of Burmese government. Today, in the jungles of the Karen State, guerrilla warfare is a fact of life.

The Shan State lies in the hill country near China, Laos, and Thailand. Buddhism influences daily life, and social activities are centered on monasteries and pagodas. The Shan believe that spirits guide, reward, and punish them. They follow a strict social order and usually live together in extended family units. The Shans speak a language related to Thai, and their alphabet is derived from Sanskrit. The people farm rice, vegetables, soybeans, and fruit. Some men work as loggers or miners, or the government conscripts them for roadwork and other forms of forced labor.

People in the Shan State suffered under Burma's military government. The military repeatedly destroyed their villages and confiscated their property. Thousands of Shan have been forced into refugee camps along the Thai border. In 1947, the Shan, along with the Chin and the Kachin, joined Aung San in signing the Panglong Agreement, which granted the Shan autonomy. They have never received their independence, however, and their conflict with the government continues.

There are several groups living in the Shan State. Among them are the Wa, a tribe with strong ties to China. Their land is remote—harsh, steep hills limit connection with the outside world. Some Wa are animists, while a few others are Buddhists or Christians. Until the 1970s, some Wa were headhunters who mounted their victims' severed heads on doorways and gates to ward off bad spirits and to appeal for a good harvest. The Wa's land is very difficult to farm, as the soil is poor and the terrain is hilly and rocky. To compensate for the fact that farmers cannot grow enough rice for their families, a large number of Wa earn money by growing opium poppies or making methamphetamine pills called *yaba* ("crazy medicine").

There are 20,000 Wa soldiers in the United Wa State Army (USWA). With Chinese-made guns and surface-to-air missiles, the USWA fiercely defends its drug trade. The U.S. State Department declares that the Wa are the world's "most heavily armed narco-traffickers." According to a *Time* magazine report Wa drug lords are encouraged to use their money to develop real estate, to run Burmese banks, to fund the Burmese army, and to control a state airline.

North of the Shan State lies the Kachin State, which is made up of villages, farms, and large plantations. Agriculture is the main activity in this region. Farmers burn forests to clear the way for fields of rice, corn, vegetables, and tobacco. Some people grow opium. During the winter, the Kachin tend livestock and fish and hunt game for food.

The Kachin wear colorful traditional dress. Women wear large earrings, as well as skirts and jackets decorated with intricate embroidery and silver buttons. Men wear purple or green longyis and often carry swords. Extended families are closely knit, and a clan system keeps society unified. Most Kachins are Baptists, converted from spirit worship by nineteenth-century missionaries. In 1960, the Kachin formed the Kachin Independence Army in order to resist a new law proclaiming Buddhism as the state religion.

The majority tribe in Rakhine State is the Arakanese, who are related to Tibetans and other Himalayan people. The Arakanese are farmers and fishers, and they cultivate pearls for the government. Their dialect is substantially unlike official Burmese, but they dress in traditional Burmese garments.

More than 700,000 other people living in Rakhine State are devout Muslims. Mosques are the mainstay of every village, and children attend school in madrassas. Men worship together in public, and women usually wear a hijab and worship at home. Their language is a mixture of Urdu, Hindi, and Arabic. Since 1991, more than 200,000 Burmese Muslims have fled Burma to live in refugee camps in neighboring Bangladesh. The United Nations supplies food to the camps regularly, but children receive only rudimentary schooling, and there is little work available for adults. Some refugees have been repatriated, but many more are in hiding.

Many tribal groups comprise the Karenni people. Experts think these tribes migrated to Burma from Mongolia in 700 BCE. Like their forebears, the Karenni are a fiercely independent people who governed themselves throughout most of Burmese history, even during the British colonial period. In 1948, however, the Burmese government included the Karenni State in the Union of Burma, much against the people's will. The Karenni tribes are very cooperative, especially when resisting outsiders' interference with their lives.

The Mon were the first ethnic group to migrate to Burma. Relatives of the Khmer in Cambodia, the Mon arrived between 2500 and 1500 BCE. By tradition, the Mon are farmers as well as peaceful Buddhists. In 1948, however, the people formed an army, the Mon People's Front (MPF), to fight for independence from the Burmese central government. The battle has been bitter, as Burmese army forces have raped and executed many Mon people, committed them to forced labor, confiscated their farmland, burned many homes, and ravaged entire villages. Many Mon have gone into hiding, with little hope that it will ever be safe to return to their homes.

The Chin tribe lives in a mountainous region called Chinland, which borders Central Burma, the Rakhine State, and India. The land is rich in plant and animal life. The Chin grow orchids, and their rhododendron-covered forests harbor tigers, elephants, monkeys, wild boar, barking deer, wild goats, and an array of birds. The Chin are composed of at least sixty individual tribes, all of which are descended from the people of central China. Each tribe has its own dialect, but most Chin speak Burmese.

The Chin have rich traditions in folktales and storytelling. They once were animists who believed in spirits. Today, however, the Chin State is the only Burmese state that is predominately Christian. Baptist missionaries, who arrived in Chinland in the nineteenth and early twentieth centuries, replaced folktales with Bible stories and encouraged the Chin to do away with their altars and sacred animal fetishes. When the British arrived, they recruited the Chin as soldiers partly because they had been educated by English-speaking missionaries and were both trustworthy and hardworking.

DIVERSITY AND UNITY

According to General Aung San and Aung San Suu Kyi, Burma's diversity should not prevent the nation from becoming a united democracy. Prior to the pact granting independence in 1948, Aung San insisted that the Burmese should set aside their differences to benefit the whole country. He said, "A nation is a conglomeration of races and religions that should develop a nationalism that is common with the welfare of one and all, irrespective of race, religion, class, or sex." He believed that a strong military was necessary to keep the country unified.

The official position of the junta had been that there are 135 races or tribes living in Burma, and it is impossible to appease each one. So in 1949, with the intent of staving off any more unrest, Prime Minister U Nu appointed Ne Win commander in chief (*tatmadaw*) of the armed forces, directing him to form a "caretaker government" that would prevent the states from seceding from the Union of Burma.

Bogyoke Aung San was the Burmese delegate to London who signed the agreement granting Burma independence.

General Ne Win was no peacemaker—he suspended the constitution, retracted the Panglong Agreement, arrested ethnic leaders and politicians, and abolished newspapers and political parties. With full executive, legislative, and judicial powers, General Ne Win plunged Burma into geopolitical isolation, social mayhem, and economic darkness. Aung San Suu Kyi would later condemn him. In an article by journalist Edward Klein, she was quoted as saying,

Ne Win is the one who caused this nation to suffer.

CHAPTER THREE

Coming Full Circle

THE BURMESE PEOPLE RARELY USE SURNAMES and usually have very short names. Aung San Suu Kyi's parents wanted to honor their family, however, so they combined her father's name (Aung San), her mother's name (Kyi), and her grandmother's name (Suu). The family members were filled with joy to share their names with a baby girl, who would one day become an international symbol of courage and a Burmese national heroine. Born on June 19, 1945, Aung San Suu Kyi arrived just after her family had spent months fraught with fear.

In March 1945, Aung San's Burmese National Army severed its ties with the Japanese and joined Britain's allies. During the Japanese occupation of Burma, Aung San had become a wanted man because he and his wife, Daw Khin Kyi, had harbored numerous Burmese fugitives. After the break with the Japanese, the soldiers of the Burmese National Army (BNA) needed Aung San at their battle headquarters in the jungle near the Thai border. With threats coming from many quarters, he could not justify taking along his pregnant wife and two young sons on the mission; nor could his family safely remain in war-ravaged Rangoon. So, with Japanese fighter planes flying over their heads, Daw Khin Kyi, her sons, her sister, and five BNA soldiers disguised themselves as poor civilians and traveled by

Aung San Suu Kyi's brothers and their mother, Daw Khin Kyi, pose before a portrait of the *Bogyoke*.

sampan and riverboat to seek protection in the remote Irrawaddy Delta. To avoid Japanese patrols, they rowed their small boats out into the Bay of Bengal and landed at a tiny fishing village. Once they arrived, they heard rumors that Aung San had been killed while fighting. Two weeks later, however, someone delivered a message written by Aung San to Daw Khin Kyi. He told the refugees that it was safe to return home to Rangoon, as the Japanese had abandoned the city. The family, as well as the Burmese in Rangoon, felt an incredible sense of relief. In that spirit of hope, Aung San Suu Kyi came into the world.

Aung San Suu Kyi's family settled into relative calm. They believed that soon the political unrest would lessen and Aung San would become prime minister of a newly independent Burma. With great expectations, the family moved to an unassuming colonial villa outside Rangoon. The house at 25 Tower Road was simple but elegant, with wide porches and lush gardens. There Aung San and Daw Khin Kyi entertained diplomats and dignitaries, hosted parties, and held meetings, all under the auspices of a new beginning for the Burmese people. But when Aung San Suu Kyi was two years old, she and her brothers lost the man they called *Phay Phay* (Daddy) in a sudden act of violence.

Aung San had retired from the military to accept a civilian position in the government. After his assassination, his wife learned that because he was a civilian, he was ineligible for an army pension. Without an income for her family, Daw Khin Kyi realized it was her duty to return to work. She contacted the Rangoon General Hospital, but no one would allow the widow of such a high-ranking official to work as a nurse. Then the government offered her a position, which she accepted. Although nannies took care of Daw Khin Kyi's children, she was still a concerned and involved parent, keeping the legacy of her husband's passion alive and setting her own moral example. She was devoutly Buddhist, self-disciplined, and meticulous in manner and appearance. She imparted these qualities to her children and provided an outpouring of love and respect for their accomplishments and intellectual curiosity.

THE LADY AS A YOUNG GIRL

Aung San Suu Kyi was a spunky child, more often found playing with her brothers in the garden or by the pool rather than doing her schoolwork. She attended St. Francis, a neighborhood convent school. When she was ten, a cousin loaned her a Sherlock Holmes mystery, and before long, Suu Kyi became an avid reader and a better student. Suu Kyi's adoring aunt—who helped the nannies raise Daw Khin Kyi's children—fed her imagination with tales of the Buddha. Meanwhile, her beloved Baptist grandfather regaled her with Bible stories. When her grandfather became blind, Suu Kyi read him Burmese translations of the Christian Bible. As Suu Kyi's fondness for literature grew, she became increasingly interested in learning English.

In 1956, at the age of eleven, Aung San Suu Kyi transferred from St. Francis to the highly regarded Methodist English High School in Rangoon. Unlike the two Catholic high schools in Rangoon, the Methodist school included students from a variety of religious backgrounds—Buddhist, Chinese Tao, Hindu, and Muslim. The school was coeducational and bilingual, and it offered degrees that qualified students for both Burmese and British universities.

Aung San Suu Kyi excelled in arts and literature classes but found math and science more difficult. Yet she met the challenge of all her studies and was often first in her class. Although she was the child of the nation's most famous man, Suu Kyi blended into the school's population well. It helped that many of her classmates were also children of well-known officials. Each time Suu Kyi received academic recognition, it was entirely due to her own initiative and talent rather than any form of favoritism.

Home life for Suu Kyi was one of gentility and privilege. Well-educated and politically influential people were frequent visitors to her mother's parlor. Daw Khin Kyi impressed upon her children—especially her daughter—the importance of a manicured appearance and respectful manners as befitting a Buddhist and a child of a revered national figure. Their lifestyle was refined but not ostentatious; their household furnishings were practical and well made; and their clothing was traditional rather than Westernized. Typical dress for Aung San Suu Kyi and her mother included a fitted white blouse and a long, patterned Burmese longyi. They wore sandals on their feet and placed fresh flowers in their hair each day.

LEAVING HOME

At age fifteen, when Aung San Suu Kyi was set to enter tenth grade, her mother was appointed ambassador to India. Though Suu Kyi was very involved in her studies, Daw Khin Kyi wanted her daughter to accompany her. From 1961 to 1967, the Indian government treated mother and daughter with the highest respect. Their home was a British mansion surrounded by verdant gardens. Aung San Suu Kyi attended the prestigious Lady Shri Ram College, took horseback riding and piano lessons, attended Japanese flower arranging classes, and continued her studies of Burmese and English literature.

The ambassador and her daughter were friendly with Indian prime minister Jawaharlal Nehru and Indira Gandhi and her family, as well as many foreign dignitaries. A particularly good friend was Lord Paul Gore-Booth, a former ambassador to Burma, who at the

Aung San Suu Kyi (*center*) poses with other students at Lady Shri Ram college in Delhi.

time was the British high commissioner to Delhi. Gore-Booth and his wife Patricia offered to be Aung San Suu Kyi's guardian as she prepared to leave Delhi to study at Oxford University in Britain.

INTO THE WEST

Aung San Suu Kyi arrived at Oxford University in 1964, at age nineteen. In the 1960s, Oxford was yet to become a coeducational school. Aung San Suu Kyi attended St. Hugh's, one of Oxford's women's colleges. The 1960s were a social tempest of anti-Vietnam war demonstrations, strong anti-capitalism movements, and major cultural changes. For the most part, Aung San Suu Kyi remained a demure, polite, traditional Burmese aristocrat. She continued to wear her longyi and made a point of plucking flowers from the campus gardens to place behind her ear each day. But given her underlying spirited nature, she did participate in a few youthful antics, such as sneaking out of her dormitory at night. Ultimately, however, she remained lady-like and composed. Noticing this, a classmate who later became an Oxford professor said that Aung San Suu Kyi

had a knack for putting one on one's best behavior. . . . In her company, I always felt like a better person.

An Oxford tutor, similarly impressed, said that Aung San Suu Kyi was very composed and self-aware, and she acted "in the manner of an instinctive thoroughbred . . . neither shy nor timid."

During most summer breaks, Aung San Suu Kyi went to India or Burma to visit her mother. One summer, however, she joined a family friend, Ma Than E, who was working for the United Nations (UN) at the time. That summer, 1965, the UN assigned Ma Than E to a newly independent Algeria. The country was in flux. In the capital of Algiers, the people were jubilant but impoverished, and much of their city was in ruins. Aung San Suu Kyi volunteered to work in UN aid tasks, such as distributing food and building homes for soldiers' widows. She saw firsthand how a colony can rebuild itself after achieving independence.

Returning to St. Hugh's College, Aung San Suu Kyi prepared for her final examinations. At the time she lived with the Gore-Booths.

Lady Gore-Booth described her charge as "a perfect guest, another daughter." In this role, Suu Kyi acquired twin "brothers," David and Christopher. The Gore-Booth twins were close friends with another set of identical twins, Michael and Anthony Aris. Often a visitor at the Gore-Booth home, Michael Aris, a student of Asian studies, fell in love with Aung San Suu Kyi. And although Suu Kyi had always insisted that she would return home and marry a Burmese man, she could not resist their mutual attraction.

Michael Aris and his twin had been born in Havana, Cuba, where his father had served as a British representative to Cuba. After their time in Cuba, the family moved to Peru before returning to England.

The husband of Aung San Suu Kyi, Professor Michael Aris, stands in front of his Oxford home. Dying of cancer in 1999, he had hoped to visit his wife one last time. The government refused to grant his visa.

Michael had attended Catholic schools in both countries, and once in England, he and his brother went to the Worth School, run by Benedictine monks. Michael was drawn to religious teaching, not in a Christian orthodox way, but rather from a spiritual, world religion frame of reference. One day, his father returned home from a trip to India with a Tibetan prayer wheel that he had bought from a Tibetan monk fleeing Chinese soldiers. The prayer wheel sparked Michael's interest in Asian religion and spirituality. In school, at Durham College, Michael focused his religious studies in the Buddhist Himalayan countries of Tibet, Bhutan, and Nepal.

In Burmese society, a relationship or marriage between a Burmese woman of Suu Kyi's social stature and a British man was unthinkable. Though very much attracted to one another, they did not act impulsively. After graduation, Aris was offered access to Bhutan's royal and monastic libraries. For a scholar of Asian religion, this was an extraordinary opportunity. His only hesitation was that it would take him away from the company of Suu Kyi for six years. But he chose to go.

Although Suu Kyi did not receive superlative marks in her Oxford finals, she was accepted into a graduate program at New York University. She left Britain and the Gore-Booths and moved in with Ma Than E, who had begun working at the UN headquarters in New York City. For three years, Suu Kyi and Ma Than E lived together.

After a year, Suu Kyi postponed her studies to take a job on an advisory committee at the United Nations. She had a low-level position, but she devoted herself to the world's leading humanitarian organization. U Thant, a countryman who had known Aung San, was secretary-general of the UN. Given U Thant's personal connection with her father, as well as Suu Kyi's friendship with Ma Than E, Suu Kyi was often invited to Sunday luncheons at the secretary-general's home. U Thant was fond of Suu Kyi, but the Burmese delegates to the UN were appointees of General Ne Win's military regime. There was much animosity between Suu Kyi and the Burmese diplomats, but she maintained her composure while upholding her political opinions. After one tense encounter, Ma Than E wrote,

being the daughter of General Aung San and Daw Khin Kyi, she could not be taken down.

While Aung San Suu Kyi worked at the UN, she volunteered in New York City hospitals and food banks. She was stunned to witness the poverty of people living in the world's wealthiest country. Far from her elite upbringing, on the back streets and alleyways of New York, Aung San Suu Kyi met people who altered her view of the world. She took more notice of people's suffering and sought to learn what she could about civil rights by studying the life and works of Dr. Martin Luther King Jr.

During her stay in New York, Suu Kyi continued to correspond with Michael Aris. By 1970, he had been gone for three years. His work was stimulating, and Asian academics were receiving it well. When Aris left Bhutan for a short vacation home to Britain, he decided to go by way of New York City. On that visit, Aris and Suu Kyi became engaged and planned to marry when Aris's work was complete. Aris returned to Bhutan, and Suu Kyi promised to visit him the following year. On Aris's next trip home for Christmas, the couple went ahead and got married. Suu Kyi resigned from the United Nations and followed her husband to Bhutan.

The wedding took place on January 1, 1972, in the home of Lord and Lady Gore-Booth. It was a bittersweet celebration. The Burmese ambassador showed his disapproval of a Burman-British marriage by refusing the invitation. Aung San Suu Kyi's favorite brother had drowned as a young boy, and her surviving brother lived in the United States. She and her brother were not close, and he did not attend the ceremony—nor, surprisingly, did Daw Khin Kyi. Daw Khin Kyi felt that her husband, Suu Kyi's father, had dedicated his life to being free of British rule, and Suu Kyi's decision to marry an Englishman was too much to bear.

Suu Kyi loved her husband very much, but she also kept alive a deep love of her native country. As a precondition of marriage, Suu Kyi had requested that Aris understand her sense of obligation to Burma:

 I only ask one thing, that should my people need me, you would help me do my duty by them.

The transition to married life was not easy. Aris's project did not provide the couple with a generous income, and the capital of Bhutan had a very low standard of living. Up to this point, Suu Kyi had never realized how much of her life she had lived in relative luxury, but despite the challenges, she accepted the change in circumstances with grace. Soon after Suu Kyi moved with Aris to Bhutan, the small kingdom joined the United Nations. She immediately found work consulting for the government on UN relations.

In late 1972, Aung San Suu Kyi and Aris returned to London and bought a small flat. Aris pursued a doctorate in Tibetan studies.

In 1973, Suu Kyi gave birth to their first child, Alexander Myint San Aung Aris. Soon after Alexander's birth, the University of California asked Aris to lead an academic expedition to Nepal. Suu Kyi and the baby accompanied him to Nepal via Burma, on what would be Suu Kyi's first visit to her native country in several years. In Burma, a family friend encouraged Daw Khin Kyi to make peace with her daughter and new son-in-law. When Daw Khin Kyi met Aris and her new grandson, she felt she had no choice: they were her family, and she gave them her blessing.

Four years later, the Aris family once again lived in a small, cramped flat near Oxford. In 1977 they had had another son, Kim, named after a character in a Rudyard Kipling novel. Having temporarily abandoned her own career ambitions, Suu Kyi was anxious to return to school. She took a part-time position cataloging Burmese literature at the university library, which afforded her many trips to Burma. While in Burma, university colleagues often urged her to return home and help counteract the influence of General Ne Win. Yet Suu Kyi chose to remain in England and be the wife of a British scholar.

Suu Kyi applied to Oxford in hopes of earning a second degree in English literature. Her past grades went against her, and she was not accepted. She turned to writing guidebooks about Nepal, Bhutan, and Burma, and also penned a biography of her father. She applied to a doctoral program in Burmese political history and was again rejected. At last she applied to do research on Burmese literature, and for that she was enthusiastically accepted, as her language skills were exceptional. Once in the program, she applied to the Center for Southeast Asian Studies (CSEAS) in Kyoto, Japan, and won an eight-month scholarship.

Aung San Suu Kyi was excited about the opportunity to investigate her father's involvement with Japan and its military, but upon

Aung San Suu Kyi's husband, Dr. Aris, and their two sons, Kim and Alexander. In 2010, Kim was granted a visa to visit his mother, seeing her for the first time after a forced separation of ten years.

arrival neither she nor her son Kim received a warm welcome. As a foreigner who did not speak Japanese, Kim was bullied at school. Outside her immediate classes, the Japanese ostracized Aung San Suu Kyi as well. Some Japanese men were chauvinistic and disapproved of Suu Kyi's independence. People held her nationality against her, and she stuck out as the daughter of Aung San and a glaring reminder of the failure of Japan's army in the hands of the Western allies and Burma.

Suu Kyi did have a few friends in Kyoto. Two of her friends were Burmese students—one a traditional Burman who repeatedly praised her father, and the other an outspoken Burmese Muslim. Together, they had many lively discussions about Burmese culture. Suu Kyi and the Muslim student often agreed passionately about Burma's need for multicultural harmony.

In 1987, Michael and Suu Kyi and their sons were home together again in England. Both Suu Kyi and Aris pursued their academic professions with enthusiasm. But one evening, on March 30, 1988, the telephone rang. Aris recalled,

I had a premonition that our lives would change forever.

Suu Kyi's mother had suffered a serious stroke. When Suu Kyi packed her bags and left for Burma, she did not know that she might never return to England.

CHAPTER FOUR

Revolution of the Spirit

A UNG SAN SUU KYI BELIEVES THAT BURMA'S best path to good government can be found in the teachings of the Buddha. In her essay "In Quest of Democracy," she writes, " . . . to provide the people with the protective coolness of peace and security, rulers must follow the teachings of the Buddha." According to Buddhist philosophy, rulers do not have god-given rights to act as they please. Rather, they must uphold codes of conduct that reflect the Buddhist virtues of honor and respect. Among these codes are the Ten Duties of Kings, the Seven Safeguards against Decline, the Four Assistances to the People, the Six Attributes of Leaders, and the Four Ways to Overcome Peril.

Suu Kyi describes the Ten Duties of Kings as follows: liberality, morality, self-sacrifice, integrity, kindness, austerity, non-anger, nonviolence, forbearance, and non-opposition to the will of the people. Each duty carries specific requirements. For example, liberality requires a ruler to contribute generously to the welfare of the people and to guard the economic security of the state. The duty of kindness leads the ruler to make "no distinction between citizen and son." Austerity means that rulers should keep simple habits and avoid excess. The seventh, eighth, and ninth duties relate to anger. A ruler should avoid any personal feelings of anger or antagonism and should deal

After her release from nineteen months of house arrest in 2002, Aung San Suu Kyi kneels in prayer at the Shwedagon Pagoda.

wisely and generously with those in opposition. The tenth duty validates democracy as the ideal form of government.

Aung San Suu Kyi writes that a legitimate government is

 founded on the consent of the people, who may withdraw their mandate at any time if they lose confidence in the ability of the ruler to serve their best interests.

In other words, citizens have the right to vote their leaders in and out of office as they see fit. Aung San Suu Kyi believes that if the Burmese government adhered to the traditional values of the Ten Duties of Kings, it would encourage prosperity, rule with just laws, and show respect for its citizens and the international community. A government such as this would be mightier than any "all-powerful ruler."

Dharma is the Buddhist system of laws and basic truths. According to Aung San Suu Kyi, laws that follow dharma guarantee human rights, which are the "foundation of peace and security." She says, "The true measure of the justice of a system is the amount of protection it guarantees to the weakest." After her experience in New York City, Aung San Suu Kyi decided that basic human rights had to be a part of government and political actions. Voting rights alone, she came to believe, would not be enough to create a strong and unified Burma. She says that ordinary Burmese simply want to "go about [their] own business freely and peacefully . . . to live a tranquil, dignified existence free from want or fear." People are not animals from the jungle, she declares, but rather are "men with reason." The Burmese believe that Buddhism elevates humans above all other creatures, for they are the only beings that can aspire to spiritual enlightenment. For a government in a Buddhist country to mistreat its citizens is appalling in its irony.

In an interview, Aung San Suu Kyi said that when the United Nations adopted the Universal Declaration of Human Rights in 1948, it was because the world had suffered "utter devastation from World War II and the denial of human rights." She thought it was encouraging that "peoples and countries decided it was time to try to stop the same kind of disaster from ever befalling the planet again." But in Burma, she claims, the military rulers had become despots, treating citizens as if they were mindless, faceless, and helpless—people to be "manipulated at will."

In her speech "Freedom from Fear," Suu Kyi says,

> **It is not enough merely to call for freedom, democracy and human rights. There has to be a united determination to persevere in the struggle, to make sacrifices in the name of enduring truths, to resist the corrupting influences of desire, ill will, ignorance and fear.**

Suu Kyi became angry when the Burmese demanded their civil rights and the government scoffed at their demands and called democracy and human rights an affectation of the West that is alien to traditional Burmese values. Lorne Craner, an assistant to former U.S. secretary of state Colin Powell, supported Suu Kyi's view. According to Craner, the Burmese military government's attitude was a "disregard for human rights and democracy [that] extends to every conceivable category of violation."

UNITING THE MANY TRIBES OF BURMA

Aung San Suu Kyi is aware that she is not only a member of the majority ethnic group, the Burmans, but also a member of her nation's ruling class. Just as her father believed, when he signed the Panglong Agreement, she believes that Burmans and the other ethnic groups must unify in order to create a free and independent Burma. Aung San Suu Kyi is shouldering the responsibility to reach out to her fellow Burmans and encourage them to accept the differences of the minority groups. She believes this is the only way to gain freedom and to develop a true, working democracy. On Union Day, 2000, Aung San Suu Kyi said,

> I greatly thank all ethnic nationalities for standing firmly with us in the struggle to achieve democracy. They are genuine friends. We must not forget this gratitude.
> If we continue to build understanding with them and obtain unity, I firmly believe that we could establish the type of union that we now wish to build. Actually, I see this Union Day as a "Nationality Day" because of the very important role of the nationalities in the Panglong Conference. All those who have studied history know this well. The Panglong Agreement emerged only because the nationalities decided to cooperate with Burmese leaders. Therefore, in principle, today is Ethnic Nationality Day.

Buddhist monks, called *sangha,* have traditionally served as teachers and mentors to the Burmese people and advisers to Burmese kings and rulers. When the British arrived, they stripped the monks of that role. Furthermore, the British encouraged Christian missionaries to spread out into the rural areas and convert the people, and this act widened the social divide. Thus, the people of Burma became separated not only by ethnic groups and economic means, but also by religion.

For centuries, the Burmese had relied on the monks to draw on Buddhist values to help them interpret modern events, but their society was changing. So when the twentieth-century democracy movement began to take hold in Burma, the sangha immediately

Many monks are very active in pro-democracy and human rights causes. Here, a Burmese Buddhist monk reads a political article in the local newspaper.

recognized how it fit into Buddhist teaching and thought. The sangha were enthusiastic about democratic principles of elected government, human rights, equal justice, and personal freedom. Since the struggle for independence in Aung San's time, the monks have been a part of the process of uniting the Burmese toward a common goal. Aung San Suu Kyi wrote that the sangha's teachings go "right through Burmese society from urban intellectuals and small shopkeepers to doughty village grandmothers."

SONGS OF FREEDOM

Each year the Burmese celebrate the Buddhist New Year with a four-day purification festival called the Water Festival, or Thingyan. During the festival, people visit pagodas and monasteries, pay respect to their elders, and perform acts of charity. They set up pavilions where they sing, dance, put on plays, feast on traditional foods, and spray each other with scented water—or, as times have changed, with hoses, water guns, and water balloons. Another important practice during Thingyan is a tradition of singing and chanting called Thangyat. Thangyat chants are likened to rap songs in which people express their sorrow and anger over the year's misfortunes and complain about poverty, hunger, and controversial political acts. In pro-democracy circles, Thangyat chants have become songs of political protest.

In 1988, Burma's military junta banned the practice and threatened to jail anyone found singing or performing protest songs. The ban sent the Thangyat tradition underground. Protest singers and comedians living in Burma continue to risk their lives for their art as they perform on subjects such as the junta's falsifying elections, imprisoning Aung San Suu Kyi, and abandoning farmers and peasants devastated by the 2008 cyclone Nargis. Burmese exiles are also keeping the Thangyat tradition alive. They broadcast protest songs into Burma, where citizens listen on their secret radios. Others have made CDs to distribute to sympathetic listeners around the world.

In 2006, Aung San Suu Kyi walked through her gate to visit with Thangyat-chanting revelers in a pavilion set up near her home. Soldiers assembled behind her. She kept walking and did not look back. Her bodyguard later asked her why she did not look back, and she replied,

 When they call out your name, you don't look back. You do what you have to do. A soldier might shoot at you, but looking back will make you feel something. That feeling may cause you to lose sight of your ultimate goal.

CHAPTER FIVE

Truth to Power

THE BURMA THAT AUNG SAN SUU KYI returned to was a country almost unrecognizable from the one she left behind as a girl. Burma—or Myanmar, as the military rulers had renamed it—was in the grip of a repressive and corrupt military regime. Since General Ne Win had come to power, the Burmese people had been shut away from the rest of the world. Only military personnel and government cronies had adequate housing and the ability to buy necessary goods and services. Throughout the nation there were ethnic uprisings, extraordinary poverty, terror, and environmental devastation. The government followed a doctrine they called the Four Cuts—a program that attempted to cut off food, money, information, and military support for any ethnic army. Without local protection, villagers were unable to fend off government raids on their livelihoods and personal property. The junta extracted natural resources and sold them to China, Russia, and India. The profits stoked only the government's coffers. The military also took over farmers' fields, destroyed villages, forced men into labor, raped women, and tortured or imprisoned anyone who spoke out.

Though stunned by the changes, Aung San Suu Kyi first set out to care for her ailing mother at Rangoon General Hospital. She noticed that many of the patients were students being

The late chairman of the Burmese Socialist Program Party, General Ne Win, on a visit to China, one of the few nations that has maintained friendly relations with Burma.

treated for serious bruises and gunshot wounds. This struck her as disturbing and suspicious. When her mother was able to leave the hospital, Aung San Suu Kyi brought Daw Khin Kyi to their old family home at 54 University Avenue on Inya Lake in Rangoon.

Soon Aung San Suu Kyi learned why there had been so many young patients in the hospital that summer. In July of 1998, General Ne Win suddenly declared that he planned to leave office. Countless thousands of Burmese, from monks and students in Rangoon to rice farmers in remote hill towns, voiced their hope that his departure would set them free from government corruption and cruelty. During what was called Democracy Summer, demonstrators filled the streets of Rangoon and called for peace and free elections. In her speech "Freedom from Fear," Aung San Suu Kyi says the government of Ne Win "had turned the country into an economic shambles. But it was more than the difficulties of eking out a barely acceptable standard of living. . . . [I]t was also the humiliation of a way of life disfigured by corruption and fear." On television, General Ne Win warned, "If in the future there are mob disturbances, if the army shoots, it hits—there is no firing into the air to scare." On August 8, 1988 (8-8-88, a date ironically considered to be extremely auspicious), the *Tatmadaw* (armed forces) began a four-day massacre, in which the military fired into crowds and killed more than ten thousand people across the country.

Taking in this horror, Aung San Suu Kyi recalled these words of Jawaharlal Nehru: "The greatest gift for an individual or a nation is . . . fearlessness." For those in Rangoon who felt overwhelmed by the government's actions, Aung San Suu Kyi urged the people to remain resolute in their beliefs and stressed the idea that truth, justice, and compassion are often the only defenses against "ruthless power." She said that General Ne Win's government had created a

Burmese soldiers suppress a 1998 pro-democracy demonstration in Rangoon.

system of fear that denied basic human rights—fear of imprisonment, torture, poverty, isolation, and loss of family, friends, property,
and livelihood. On August 26, 1988, Aung San Suu Kyi stood in front
of Rangoon General Hospital and announced that she would take a
stand and speak at a rally on August 28 at the Shwedagon Pagoda.

She said on that day,

**Reverend monks and people! This public rally
is aimed at informing the whole world of the
will of the people . . . the keenest desire for a
multiparty democratic system of government.**

Speaking from the temple steps, she praised the students who had made the rally possible. Nearly 500,000 had gathered that day to hear the words of encouragement spoken by Bogyoke Aung San's daughter. Suu Kyi called it her duty, as her father's daughter, to help transform Burma in any way she could. Suspecting that many in the crowd felt unsure of her commitment, Aung San Suu Kyi admitted that although she had married a foreigner and had lived out of the country for a long time, it hadn't lessened her love for and devotion to her country "by any measure or degree."

Aung San Suu Kyi spoke of many other things that day. She described how the people were growing stronger and that their "cherished aims" were drawing near, but she also cautioned them to be nonviolent and disciplined. Together, she said, they shared responsibility for the great task at hand, and they needed to be unified in their desires. She called out for a multiparty government, free and fair elections, and most important, a society whose people let no "divisions creep in." Aung San Suu Kyi told the crowd that their future actions were, in effect, the "second struggle for Burmese independence."

Immediately after the rally, there seemed to be an evolving sense that free elections and a new Burmese awakening could be possible. Demonstrations continued. But on September 18, 1988, the government gave control to nineteen officers who formed an agency called the State Law and Order Restoration Council (SLORC). SLORC immediately put a hammerlock on public demonstrations and sent the Tatmadaw into the streets to contain the unrest. Thousands were tortured, imprisoned, or killed, and more than ten thousand students escaped to the hill country or the border areas. Others fled the country altogether. Amnesty International, an organization defending the rights of political prisoners around the world, estimates that around 1,500 political prisoners from that time remain in jail to this day.

On August 26, 1988, Aung San Suu Kyi delivers her first public pro-democracy speech on the steps of the Shwedagon Pagoda before hundreds of thousands of Burmese citizens.

After the protests, Ne Win lost control of the government. His replacement was another general named Saw Maung. General Saw Maung placed Burma under martial law and declared a state of emergency. He also nullified the Burmese Constitution and abruptly changed the name of the country to the Union of Myanmar.

After the SLORC crackdown in September, the council created a new political party called the National Unity Party (NUP) and, in a surprise move, declared that Burma would hold a national election. SLORC invited any other groups interested in participating in the election to form a political party and to register right away.

EXCERPTS FROM "FREEDOM FROM FEAR"

AUNG SAN SUU KYI, 1990

It is not power that corrupts but fear. Fear of losing power corrupts those who wield it and fear of the scourge of power corrupts those who are subject to it.

It is true that years of incoherent policies, inept official measures, burgeoning inflation, and falling real income had turned the country into an economic shambles. But it was more than the difficulties of eking out a barely acceptable standard of living that had eroded the patience of a traditionally good-natured, quiescent people—it was also the humiliation of a way of life disfigured by corruption and fear.

Where there are no such [just] laws, the burden of upholding the principles of justice and common decency falls on ordinary people.

It is not enough merely to call for freedom, democracy, and human rights. There has to be a united determination to persevere in the struggle, to make sacrifices in the name of enduring truths, to resist the corrupting influences of desire, ill will, ignorance, and fear.

At the root of human responsibility is the concept of perfection, the urge to achieve it, the intelligence to find a path towards it, and the will to follow that path if not to the end at least the distance needed to rise above individual limitations and environmental impediments. It is man's vision of a world fit for rational, civilized humanity which leads him to dare and to suffer to build societies free from want and fear. Concepts such as truth, justice, and compassion cannot be dismissed as trite when these are often the only bulwarks which stand against ruthless power.

Saw Maung's thinking was that with numerous parties on the ballot to choose from, the NUP would easily win most of the seats in the parliament.

In the end, 234 parties registered. Among them was the National League for Democracy (NLD). Executive members of the NLD included Aung San Suu Kyi, several former army officers who were now opposed to the ruling military government, and many prominent democratic political leaders. Aung San Suu Kyi was appointed general secretary. She led dozens of meetings at her home in Rangoon, organized the campaign, and enlisted supporters from numerous ethnic and political interest groups. She proved to be persistent and persuasive like her father, and gracious and thoughtful like her mother.

In December 1988, Daw Khin Kyi's health deteriorated rapidly. She died in her home on University Avenue on December 27. Suu Kyi was devastated at losing the only parent she had ever really known. A funeral was planned for January 2, 1989, and in a rare instance of generosity, the government granted visas for Suu Kyi's husband and children, as well as her estranged brother from the United States, to attend the funeral. (As it was unusual for SLORC to grant visas, some speculated that government leaders did so to encourage Suu Kyi to leave Burma and return with her family to England, now that her mother had passed away.)

On the day of the funeral, thousands of citizens gathered in the streets to pay their respects. SLORC leaders, including Saw Maung, met with Suu Kyi in her home. She was concerned that her mother's funeral could become an opportunity for confrontation. Soldiers surrounded the city, but for the first time since September 1988, large numbers of people gathered in public without incident. The crowd was peaceable and orderly, and the soldiers had no excuse for violence. After the funeral, Michael, Alexander, and Kim Aris left without Aung San Suu Kyi. Junta officials were extremely displeased and set about making plans to dampen her popularity and to upset her political aims.

The NLD mapped out a plan to campaign throughout the country. Although SLORC had outlawed the right of assembly, Aung San Suu Kyi and her most trusted colleagues ventured into the nation's outlying regions to gain support and to call for unity and democracy. As Aung San Suu Kyi and fellow members of the NLD ventured into ethnic towns and villages, government soldiers closely followed them. The soldiers did not deny people their right to assemble, but they kept their guns aimed at Suu Kyi's entourage. To disrupt the throngs of people who gathered at Suu Kyi's rallies, soldiers blared music from loudspeakers to drown out her words. They told people not to congregate in public places, lean out windows, or wave flags when her motorcade passed by.

As tensions increased, soldiers took to firing shots into the air over crowds and blocking off streets with sandbags and barbed wire. On April 5, 1989, in a town near Mandalay, soldiers were commanded to aim their guns at Suu Kyi. They stood in front of the NLD's cars to prevent them from driving to a meeting, so Suu Kyi got out of her car to walk. A captain caught up with her, and she turned to ask him if he was preparing to arrest her. He said no, and she continued on to her meeting. Along the way, Suu Kyi walked over to a line of soldiers with their guns aimed in her direction and started to talk about democracy and freedom. The soldiers abruptly opened their blockade and allowed the cars to pass. She wrote later to her husband that she could not let herself leave that town until she was assured that there would be "fair play."

Back in Rangoon, Aung San Suu Kyi and the NLD planned a peaceful pro-democracy march for July 19, 1989. This day, which was known as Martyr's Day, commemorated the day Aung San and the other government ministers were assassinated. Aris and the couple's sons planned to travel to Burma to attend the event. The boys arrived, but Aris remained in Europe to attend his father's funeral.

Meanwhile, Aung San Suu Kyi knew that SLORC was increasing its oppressive tactics against political gatherings. Concerned, she opted to cancel the march and planned to visit her father's grave alone with her sons. Dozens of NLD supporters were with Aung San Suu Kyi and her boys on the morning of July 20 when her home was surrounded by Tatmadaw troops. That afternoon, two soldiers went to her door and ordered everyone but a maid, a cook, and Suu Kyi's two sons to leave, upon threat of death. Then the soldiers entered her home, rifled through her belongings, and cut the telephone line. They announced that she was under house arrest. She could not receive visitors and could no longer leave, unless it was to leave Burma altogether.

In other parts of Rangoon, many other NLD leaders were arrested, and more than two thousand democracy supporters were detained. The NLD was left without effective leadership and could no longer raise money, campaign, or make use of radio, television, or newspapers to spread its message of democracy. On July 21, Aung San Suu Kyi asked to be imprisoned along with other NLD members who had been taken to Insein Prison. Knowing there would be a public backlash against them if they granted her request, SLORC officials refused, and Aung San Suu Kyi went on a hunger strike.

Michael Aris arrived once he heard of his wife's fast. The Tatmadaw surrounded his airplane and took him into custody. Fearing that Aris would join the NLD, the generals negotiated with him. Suu Kyi did not want the NLD prisoners to be harmed. SLORC leaders again realized that if they put the Bogyoke's daughter in danger, the

Burmese would revolt. Eventually a pact was made, Aung San Suu Kyi broke her fast, and Aris and the boys left for England. On December 22, 1989, while still under arrest, Suu Kyi submitted her application to be a candidate in the upcoming election. She wrote that she wished "to honor the courage and perseverance of the people who are striving for democracy and . . . to help fulfill the just aspirations of the people to the best of my ability."

Even with Aung San Suu Kyi under house arrest and many NLD party members intimidated by SLORC, 82 percent of Burmans cast their ballot. Against all odds, Aung San Suu Kyi's NLD won in a landslide victory—392 of 485 seats in the parliament. Ethnic minority parties opposed to the junta won sixty-five more seats. Aung San Suu Kyi was in line to become only the second prime minister of an independent Burma.

SLORC and the junta were jolted by their defeat and, in their shock, realized they were astoundingly unpopular. They acted quickly and unilaterally to negate the election. SLORC declared that the election had been held not for seats in parliament, but rather for a committee to consider drafting a new constitution. They arrested even more NLD members and clamped down harder on basic freedoms. Martial law remained in place for two years.

In 1992, General Than Shwe replaced Saw Maung as prime minister. Under his administration, many political prisoners were released and many of SLORC's laws were repealed. Plans to draft a new constitution were in the works, and the junta signed cease-fires with many ethnic armies, but the government still had no plans to return to civilian control. The Burmese passports of Suu Kyi's family were revoked, which meant that Aris and the boys could no longer visit her. And Aung San Suu Kyi remained a prisoner in her home.

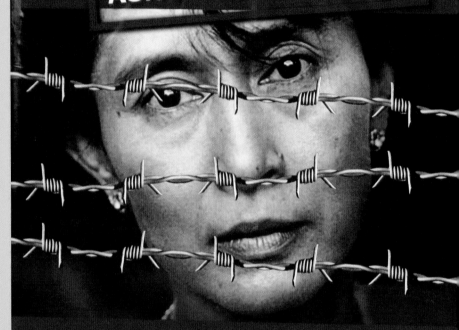

CHAPTER SIX

FREE!
AUNG SAN SUU KYI

BURMESE PRO DEMOCRATIC LEADE

The Prisoner

W HEN AUNG SAN SUU KYI WAS TAKEN prisoner, government officials refused to allow any visitors except members of her immediate family. There was to be no outside contact—no telephone, television, mail, or packages—except mail from her husband and sons. Under the provisions of martial law, Suu Kyi could be held prisoner without a trial or any formal charges for three years.

On the one-year anniversary of Aung San Suu Kyi's detention, pro-democracy protesters attempted to gather near her home on University Avenue. Soldiers immediately dispersed the crowd. In response, her supporters emblazoned Suu Kyi's face on T-shirts, banners, political buttons, and posters. Soon afterward, authorities told Suu Kyi that her sentence would be extended for five more years, again without a trial or formal charges. Furthermore, the government revoked her rights to receive mail and visits from her family.

The junta has made many controversial statements about Aung San Suu Kyi's imprisonment. Officials declared that she "endangered the state" and defended her incarceration by asserting, "Myanmar is not the only country that promulgates the laws to prevent those who pose a danger to the state."

Around the world, people protested the August 2009 sentencing of Aung San Suu Kyi to three years of imprisonment.

The government claimed it was the "parent of the people" and had exercised "great patience." Suu Kyi's supporters claimed that even according to the strict and outdated 1975 Burmese Law Safeguarding the State from Dangers of Subversive Elements, the government was holding Suu Kyi illegally. This law states that a prisoner can be held for only five years without charges or a trial. The junta countered their protests by interpreting the law to mean that Suu Kyi's prison term could be renewed five times.

OUTSIDE THE WALLS

Many political observers in Burma believe that if the NLD had not been so overwhelmingly victorious, and if Aung San Suu Kyi had not been elected to lead the new parliament, the military would have set her free soon after her arrest. They also believe that if she had not been the daughter of Bogyoke Aung San, much more harm would have come to her.

Instead, on July 27, 1990, junta officials issued Order 90/1, which declared the junta's supreme authority over the government. Its rationale was that SLORC was recognized by the United Nations, foreign governments, and other international agencies. Therefore, SLORC leaders had no obligation to relinquish power to the NLD or to any of the other political parties that had won seats in the election. SLORC spokesmen said the council planned to make a transition to a civilian government, but not before order was restored and a constitution could be drafted. They presented no timetable for such a transition and announced that rather than accepting the election winners as delegates to the constitutional convention, they would make their own selections. The first session of the constitutional convention was held on January 9, 1993. The military government chose more than 80 percent of the 702 delegates. Only eighty-six delegates were members of the NLD.

Though Aung San Suu Kyi was under house arrest, her jailers called it "restricted residence." Barbed wire surrounded her home, and signs placed along University Avenue issued orders such as "Do Not Slow Down" or "No U-Turns." Soldiers stood guard at the entrances to her home, and they detained or beat anyone who appeared to loiter in the area. Soon it was against the law to wear a badge or a T-shirt showing Suu Kyi's image. Even speaking her name was cause for punishment. In order to avoid trouble, people took to calling her simply the Lady. The government sorely wanted to make her vanish from the public eye. Yet Burmese citizens revered Suu Kyi all the more for her strength, much to the junta's chagrin. The Lady was aware that her public persona was critical for keeping the dream of democracy alive. She has said,

 If I am invisible, I am rendered irrelevant.

LIFE INSIDE

From the first days of her detention, Suu Kyi made every attempt to maintain her dignity, her focus, and her privacy. She dressed every morning in a fresh blouse and a colorful longyi. She wore lipstick and flowers in her hair. She tried, in the beginning, to tend her ample gardens and lawn. But the presence of soldiers disturbed her and invaded her privacy. She was forced to let her grounds become an overgrown shambles. Aris sent her frequent packages containing personal gifts, books, music, and videos. Government-paid photographers took images of Suu Kyi in her fine clothes with her collections of videos and music and released them to newspapers and television, so that ordinary people who were barely able to make a living might resent her for her luxuries. She asked her husband to discontinue the gifts, and her popularity rose to greater heights.

Due to her mother's influence, Aung San Suu Kyi had been familiar with Buddhist practices for most of her life. She had included Buddhist rites at her marriage. Her sons had had a Buddhist initiation ceremony. While campaigning, she had visited many pagodas and monasteries during Buddhist rituals such as lighting joss sticks and waving healing smoke. Now, as a prisoner, Suu Kyi sought out her mother's Buddhist library in the hope that Buddhism would give her comfort and stimulate her mind. She learned

Aung San Suu Kyi gazes over the fertile farmland of the Irrawaddy River Delta.

to chant sutras, which are Buddhist prayers, and began to meditate. Along with many other Burmese prisoners, she adopted the Vipassana form of meditation, which is based on mental focus and controlled, conscious breathing. When Aung San Suu Kyi was briefly released from house arrest, she told followers that her Buddhist faith had made her "spiritually stronger."

Suu Kyi paid close attention to her daily life. She rose at 4:30 a.m. to meditate. Then she listened to news radio programs such as *BBC World* and *Voice of America*. In 1992, a new radio program came on the air. Called the *Democratic Voice of Burma*, it was sponsored by the Norwegian government and staffed by Burmese exiles. After eating a light breakfast, she tended to household chores. Later in the afternoon she would play Bach concertos on an aging, out-of-tune piano. Her aunt remained in a small house on the grounds and, aside from a maid who brought her food, was the only person she was allowed to see.

Suu Kyi was no longer allowed to send or receive letters from her husband. When she had stopped the delivery of his packages, the government had responded by holding her mail. Dr. Aris said that the last letter he received from his wife was in 1990.

The government did not want Suu Kyi to have any money. Authorities insisted that they would supply her food and pay her utility bills. This was not acceptable to her, so she began selling her furniture. In truth, liaisons gave her money but actually stockpiled her furniture in a warehouse so they could return the belongings in the event that she would be released.

On July 10, 1995, a sleek, white limousine pulled up to 54 University Avenue, and out stepped the chief of police. It was six days shy of the sixth anniversary of Aung San Suu Kyi's detention. Without preamble, the chief told Suu Kyi that she was no longer under arrest.

Almost immediately, Aung San Suu Kyi called a meeting with former NLD leaders. She said they decided to

" pick up where we had left off six years ago, to continue our work.

Soon the soldiers left their posts on the street, and crowds began to form. Suu Kyi was too weak to mingle with so many people, but she climbed up on a table that had been placed near her front gate and spoke to her fellow Burmese for the first time in six years. She explained that she had promised SLORC that she would encourage "national reconciliation." To delighted cheers, she told the crowd that democracy was attainable. Each day the crowd grew larger. And each day Suu Kyi appeared at the gate, on top of her table, and spoke. Soon it became stressful and unconstructive to spend so much time speaking every day. Suu Kyi decided that she would speak only on Saturdays and Sundays. Weekends at 54 University Avenue became the most popular attraction in Rangoon. Everyone came to hear her—teachers, doctors, students, reporters, lawyers, monks, farmers, tradespeople, homemakers, the old and the young, the rich and the poor, foreigners, tourists, politicians, and diplomats. Vendors set up little stalls along the street to sell food and souvenirs. Suu Kyi hung a letter box on her gate and invited people to leave questions. Each week she did her best to answer the questions, even if they had nothing at all to do with her political views. The people loved her, and she was, in turn, buoyed by their energy.

Aung San Suu Kyi and her fellow NLD members threw themselves into efforts to enlist supporters and to challenge the government in the name of democracy. Suu Kyi had spent several years

After being released temporarily from house arrest in July 1995,
Aung San Suu Kyi addressed supporters at the entrance of her home.

meditating and developing a state of *metta*, or loving-kindness. With this sensibility, Suu Kyi felt that she would be defeated if she allowed herself to feel hatred for the regime. She told her supporters that they would be more likely to "hasten the fall" of SLORC if they used non-violence and empathy.

At first, SLORC made some overtures. The council returned Aung San Suu Kyi's title of general secretary of the NLD. They allowed her to hold meetings in her home, yet as time passed, more and more soldiers were stationed outside her gates. The junta stepped up its various forms of harassment, such as denying entry visas to her husband and her sons—even in 1999, when Aris learned that he had cancer and, at age fifty-three, had only months to live. Suu Kyi agonized over her husband's death and longed to see her sons. But she knew that if she left Burma, she would never be permitted to return. She wrote,

I dream about my family all the time, but there are a lot of people here that need to be cared about and loved and looked after. They've become my second family.

On several occasions Suu Kyi attempted to travel outside of Rangoon. The first time, soldiers of the Tatmadaw blocked her way. She refused to back down and told her driver, "Keep moving." She remained in the car until soldiers forcibly hauled her driver out of the vehicle. A month later, she was more prepared. Suu Kyi brought enough food and water for six days. Again soldiers stopped her car, and this time she held out until her supplies were gone. She continued to resist the pressure of SLORC, renamed in 1998 as the State Peace and Development Council (SPDC).

In 2000, Suu Kyi and some other members of the NLD tried to travel by train to Mandalay. When they arrived, the train station had been cleared. Only Suu Kyi and her companions were allowed to enter. The building was filled with soldiers. Outside the station, NLD supporters had been arrested. An armed guard took Aung San Suu Kyi back to her home on University Avenue. Junta officials refused to say that she was under house arrest; rather, they claimed that she was being held in her home for "her own protection." She remained there until 2002, although for a time she was allowed to conduct meetings in her home and, occasionally, to travel to some of the hill country and border states.

On May 30, 2003, Aung San Suu Kyi and a convoy of NLD members were again en route to Mandalay. Waiting to greet them were large crowds of NLD supporters, as well as government-sponsored protesters who were members of a group called the Union Solidarity and Development Association (USDA). The USDA was made up of farmers and civil servants who dared not refuse membership in the organization, for fear of losing their jobs or being forced into labor.

When the NLD motorcade passed through the streets of the village of Depayin, hundreds of armed USDA rioters surrounded it and blocked its movements. Hundreds more USDA rioters appeared out of the bushes and side streets and turned on the NLD crowd with angry threats and violence. Many people were robbed and hundreds beaten, and more than sixty people were killed. Aung San Suu Kyi's driver wanted to get her out of the melee, but she wanted to stand by the people. When shots were fired into their car, however, her driver sped away. Within earshot of the riots, Tatmadaw troops prevented their escape, surrounded their car, and arrested Aung San Suu Kyi. This time, she was detained secretly at Insein Prison for three months before being sentenced again to house arrest.

In May 2007, the government extended Aung San Suu Kyi's house arrest for another year, despite a personal appeal from UN secretary-general Kofi Annan. In August of that year, prompted by rising fuel prices, thousands of Burmese, in more than twenty cities across the country, took to the streets in protest. Tens of thousands of Buddhist monks joined them, to create the largest public demonstrations in thirty years. On September 22, one thousand monks passed through the barricades on Inya Road to stop and pray in front of Aung San Suu Kyi's home. In a rare public appearance, Suu Kyi left her home to receive the monks' blessing. The next day, she was taken to Insein Prison. The military instituted curfews around the country, and soldiers made nighttime raids on people's homes. Thousands of monks were shackled and taken to remote prisons, and hundreds more were executed.

Aung San Suu Kyi was returned to house arrest. The junta appointed a special liaison officer, General Aung Kyi, to conduct talks with Suu Kyi and the government. Natural disaster quickly overshadowed this effort toward communication, however. On May 2, 2008, a devastating tropical storm, Cyclone Nargis, slammed into the Irrawaddy Delta and ultimately killed or displaced more than 2 million people. Along with the UN, leaders in countries across Asia and in Europe, Australia, and the United States stepped forward to offer emergency aid. Saying that the victims could "stand by themselves," the junta turned away U.S. medical and supply ships. Meanwhile, a government editorial declared, "The people from Irrawaddy can survive without chocolate bars donated by foreign countries."

The fallout from the disaster increased daily, as more and more Burmese people became homeless or were found injured or dead. The junta was slow to respond to the people's needs, and in an act many viewed as callous, it prematurely dismantled refugee camps and forced survivors to clean up the mess and bury the dead in exchange for food and water.

As the world condemned the junta's reaction to the crisis, the junta relented and granted visas permitting international organizations to provide humanitarian aid. Foreign supporters of Aung San Suu Kyi and members of the NLD in Burma saw other nations' presence as an opportunity to popularize her plight and to secure her release. NLD members wearing Suu Kyi T-shirts chanted outside

Following Cyclone Nargis, Aung San Suu Kyi accused the government of being slow to act to help survivors, abandoning them to live in crude, makeshift shelters and relocation camps.

her home, "Aung San Suu Kyi. Release her immediately!" Riot police detained several of the demonstrators. On May 22, 2008, the government extended Suu Kyi's house arrest for another year. In June, the junta released a statement saying that, "Due to the crimes they have committed, they well deserve flogging punishment as in the case of naughty children."

During the disaster recovery, as foreign nations worked with the Burmese government to provide aid, the junta held the line against discussing internal politics, but its leaders slowly lifted the veil of secrecy and began to hold economic talks with foreign officials.

ESCAPE CITY

In 2005, General Than Shwe abruptly moved his government 250 miles (400 km) north of Rangoon to the hilly land
of jungle and sugarcane fields in central Burma. Initially,
the government called the new capital city Yan Lon, meaning "secure from strife." Then the government changed the
name to Naypyidaw, which means "City of Kings." Most Burmese, however, secretly think of the place as Escape City.

With barely a day's notice, the junta informed all the government workers who were single and without families that
they needed to pack their belongings and move. Employees
with families were given a little more time, as schools had
yet to be built in the new city. Built by forced laborers—many
of whom were children—Naypyidaw was developed into an
isolated expanse of wide roads—good for accommodating
tanks—with mansions and golf courses for the elite, impos-
ing government buildings, and little else. According to Aung
Zaw, editor of *Irrawaddy Magazine*, the city has become surrounded by missile silos, escape tunnels, and anti-aircraft
guns. Workers' housing consisted of minimalist, Soviet-style
apartments in a restricted compound. There were no facili-
ties built to house foreign embassies. The general went so
far as to tell foreign diplomats, "If you need to communicate
on urgent matters, you can send a fax."

Government leaders claimed they had left Rangoon because it was getting too crowded. Most Burmese believe that there are numerous reasons, none of which involve crowding. Observers argue that the most probable reason, given the fortresslike construction of the new capital, is the junta's fear of attack from both external and internal forces. As the international community has demanded that the government cease human rights abuses and release political prisoners—notably Aung San Suu Kyi—the junta has grown more paranoid and defensive. The junta is not only afraid of Western nations, but also increasingly concerned about political dissidents inside the country. As one ethnic minority leader commented about Suu Kyi, "Her leadership is so gigantic and powerful that the military leaders are frightened of having put her under house arrest."

It is clear to most observers that junta leaders barricaded themselves and are preparing for any future attack. Ironically, Aung San Suu Kyi's father, General Aung San, began his Burmese independence movement in the region that is now known as Naypyidaw.

People started to sense that the political tension and government restrictions could be lessening. The government scheduled elections for 2010, and Aung San Suu Kyi and NLD leaders were hopeful that 2009 would be the last year of her house arrest. But May 6, 2009, heralded a bizarre turn of events.

On this date, John Yettaw, an American citizen from Missouri and a Vietnam War veteran with a history of instability, donned homemade swim fins and goggles, swam 2 miles (3.2 km) across Inya Lake, and came ashore on the grounds of Aung San Suu Kyi's crumbling estate. Complaining that he had diabetes and heart trouble and would likely die if she forced him to leave, he asked her to take him in for the night. After first refusing, Aung San Suu Kyi and her maids took pity on the desperate, heavyset man at their doorstep. They allowed Yettaw to stay for two nights. As Yettaw prepared to leave, soldiers guarding Suu Kyi's home spotted the intruder, and the incident escalated into an international debacle. The military arrested Suu Kyi, her two maids, and the American trespasser and took them to Insein Prison.

Aung San Suu Kyi's trial was held behind closed doors. International tensions ensued. Diplomats from foreign countries tried to intervene, and Suu Kyi's lawyers pled her innocence in vain. Suu Kyi herself said that the decision would reveal "the whole of legal, justice and constitutional system in our country."

As expected, the court convicted Aung San Suu Kyi of violating the conditions of her house arrest and sentenced her to three years of hard labor. But later, in front of an audience of foreign diplomats, General Than Shwe announced that Suu Kyi's sentence would be commuted to eighteen months of house arrest. A witness quoted in the British newspaper the *Guardian* declared that the junta had staged the announcement in "a choreographed attempt to get us to witness the leniency, clemency and humanity of the general."

The peculiarity of the Yettaw incident aroused worldwide controversy. Many people believed the junta masterminded the event in order to keep Aung San Suu Kyi under arrest past the date of the 2010 elections. As evidence of their theory, they note that it is extremely difficult to obtain a visa to enter Burma, yet John Yettaw, oddly, had been granted a visa twice. Aung Lin Htut, a former Burmese military officer and deputy ambassador to the United States, added to suspicions by explaining, "There's always tight security around Inya Lake. Without help from security personnel, there's no way you could just swim across the lake." Prime Minister Gordon Brown of Britain declared, "The facade of [Suu Kyi's] prosecution is made more monstrous because its real objective is to sever her bond with the people for whom she is a beacon of hope and resistance."

After the trial, Aung San Suu Kyi spoke briefly to the diplomats and thanked them for being present at her trial. In her gracious, ever-hopeful manner, she said,

I look forward to working together for the future prosperity of my country.

CHAPTER SEVEN

The World Stage

O N AUGUST 28, 1988, WHEN AUNG SAN SUU KYI stood at the base of Shwedagon Pagoda, she forged a potent relationship not only with the Burmese people, but also with the world. Defenders of democracy have championed her cause and admired her determined but gracious resolve. Even nations that do not espouse democracy have been affected by Aung San Suu Kyi's strength and appeals for justice. As her country has become more isolated and more impoverished, she has asked the world community to come to Burma's aid, "The international community as a whole should recognize that it has got responsibilities. It can't ignore grave injustices that are going on within the borders of any particular country."

THE POLITICS OF POVERTY

Aung San Suu Kyi believed that the Burmese military government was not been "capable of running the economy." Some observers say that the junta systematically destroyed the livelihood of the people. Burma has consistently been ranked by the UN as one of the least developed Asian countries —a painful irony for a nation so endowed with freshwater, arable land, and other natural resources. Wages in Burma cannot support a family. In 2012, the average annual income of a Burmese citizen was equal to $1,817 USD. A reporter from the BBC had a rare opportunity to interview several Burmese citizens. A taxi driver told her, "I'm just surviving one day at a time" and a farmer confessed that he was lucky to make 1,000 kyats—about 80

U.S. President Barack Obama meets with Myanmar opposition leader Aung San Suu Kyi on November 19, 2012.

cents—a day. He can barely buy low-grade rice for his family, and prices keep going up. The farmer complained that people are very restricted in buying what they need, such as gas, household items, and postage stamps. Many are forced to buy goods on the black market or through the use of bribery.

Nicholas Kristof, a writer for the *New York Times*, wrote that walking across the border from Thailand to Burma was like going back fifty years. According to the World Health Organization, the junta spent nearly 50 percent of the nation's income on the military, only 8 percent on health care, and 3 percent on education. An average Burmese has less than four years of schooling. One in ten children dies before his or her fifth birthday. An estimated 90 percent of the population lives below the poverty line.

In Rangoon, the impoverished and the wealthy live side by side. Modern vehicles, big houses, and other luxuries are available to a very few, mostly military, families. In much of the city, however, ordinary Burmese go without electricity for much of the day, ride decrepit public buses, and have little access to clean water and healthy food. Ethnic groups that have alienated the junta suffer even more.

Some foreign governments, most notably China, trade with Burma, but ordinary Burmese receive little or no benefit. While in prison, Aung San Suu Kyi encouraged foreign governments to impose economic sanctions against the junta. In 1988, when the junta cracked down on pro-democracy demonstrations that left more than three thousand people dead, most countries complied with Suu Kyi's request and placed economic sanctions on Burma. In 1990, when the junta denied Aung San Suu Kyi and the NLD their election victory, Suu Kyi said,

 The sanctions have hit Burma very hard.

The junta denied the claim, and one general boasted to a foreign official, "We are not scared of Western sanctions; we will survive as long as we have rice, salt, and ngapi [fermented fish paste]." Yet for many of the 48 million poor Burmese, those simple goods are all that they have. In 1997, Suu Kyi drafted a speech asking foreign nations to continue to boycott trade with Burma, and to further isolate Burma from the rest of the world, she asked tourists to stay away. In urging other nations to adhere to sanctions Suu Kyi wrote,

 Please, use your liberty to promote ours.

Despite increased revenues from the sale of oil, gas, minerals, and other natural resources to China, India, and Russia, in 2009, the junta's leaders grew eager to see sanctions lifted. General Than Shwe suggested that the junta might talk with Aung San Suu Kyi if she were to agree to help persuade the West to lift economic sanctions. In a letter to the general on September 25, 2009, Suu Kyi wrote,

 Let me meet with the charge d'affaires of the U.S., an ambassador representing the European Union countries, and the Australian ambassador to discuss lifting sanctions against Myanmar.

In February 2010, the United Nations human rights envoy to Burma, Tomas Quintana, came to discuss the elections. He met with several junta officials and then waited until the last minute

at the airport in the hope of talking with Aung San Suu Kyi. His request was denied.

Finally, in April 2010, Aung San Suu Kyi was allowed to meet with diplomats from the United States, the United Kingdom, and Australia. The outcome of each of the sessions entailed a review of the sanctions policy. The groups decided that some sanctions could be lifted if the junta released all political prisoners and allowed opposition parties to participate in elections. Were the junta to comply, foreign investment and economic aid would be available. Suu Kyi said,

We have never made a secret of the fact that we consider international opinion of importance, because we live in a world where everyone is linked to everybody else.

Suu Kyi herself believes that her role, and her party's role, is to speak to the government and to the world for the sake of the people. She reasons,

We are a political party that represents the people of Burma. In fact, I can say that we are the only organization in Burma that has received a mandate of the people. So there is a lot that we have to do.

Aung San Suu Kyi waves to the crowd as she leaves National League for Democracy (NLD) headquarters after addressing journalists and supporters in Yangon on April 2, 2012.

ELECTIONS

The pressure of the 2010 elections generated friction throughout Burma and endangered the junta's relationships with governments around the world. Although the junta declared in 2009 that it would hold "discipline-flourishing" democratic elections, many officials said that the elections would be not only illegal, but a sham.

Burma's military government had no intention of reenacting the embarrassing 1990 landslide election win of Aung San Suu Kyi and the NLD party. So in 2008, the junta, in an effort to avert a similar outcome, drafted a new constitution and passed several restrictive election laws. In particular, the regulations called for setting aside at least 25 percent of the seats in parliament for the military. The military would also make appointments to an election commission that would conduct a final tally of the votes. Most laws seemed specifically directed at Aung San Suu Kyi. For example, one rule stated that no person can be a candidate if he or she has been arrested and convicted or has been married to— or associated with—foreign citizens. The laws also denied formal recognition of any political party that is associated with someone who is imprisoned.

Governments around the world condemned Burma's election laws. A U.S. State Department representative said the laws "make a mockery of the democratic process." In a statement in August 2009, U.S. president Barack Obama said,

"

I join the international community in calling for Aung San Suu Kyi's immediate, unconditional release. . . . Suppressing ideas never succeeds in making them go away.

I call on the Burmese regime to heed the views of its own people and the international community and to work towards genuine national reconciliation.

"

The British ambassador to Burma agreed with Obama and called the laws "regrettable and very disappointing." Likewise, the foreign secretary of the Philippines stated, "Unless they release Aung San Suu Kyi and allow her and her party to participate in elections, it's a complete farce and therefore contrary to [Burma's] roadmap to democracy." Alluding to the idea that Burma's election laws particularly address Aung San Suu Kyi, the Canadian foreign minister said that the laws are "a deliberate effort by Burmese military leaders to prevent legitimate democratic actors from participating in the promised elections."

Even countries that traditionally avoid interfering with Burma's internal affairs—many of which belong to the Association of Southeast Asian Nations (ASEAN)—disagreed with the laws and their impact on Aung San Suu Kyi's party. At a meeting in Hanoi, the Vietnamese prime minister said that Burma's elections should be "fair and democratic, with the participation of all parties." The government of Indonesia offered to send a delegation to oversee Burmese elections, but their offer was refused.

When the first of the new Burmese election laws became public, Aung San Suu Kyi and the NLD responded by issuing the Shwegondaing Declaration on April 29, 2009. They demanded that the Burmese government release all political prisoners, acknowledge the NLD victories in the 1990 election, and reexamine the 2008 draft constitution. Aung San Suu Kyi and the NLD rejected many of the constitution's unjust provisions, such as immunity from prosecution for crimes committed by military personnel, the lack of an independent judiciary, and the lack of equal representation in parliament. They also condemned the constitution's denial of ethnic autonomy, freedom of speech, and the right to assemble. The NLD demanded that the government recognize ethnic minorities, provide for fair elections, and create justice in the courts. Finally, they demanded that the government release Aung San Suu Kyi and engage in a sincere dialogue with her.

In March 2010, Aung San Suu Kyi and the NLD had to choose whether or not to participate in the elections. Some people felt that by participating, the party would be indicating that the electoral process and the 2008 constitution were legitimate. Others believed that by not participating, they might be shirking their responsibility to give voters an opportunity to elect democratic candidates.

In the end, the NLD announced that they would not compete in the elections. Numerous parties, including many ethnic parties, followed suit. Aung San Suu Kyi said that she was "happy" with her party's decision, even though it meant the NLD would be legally dissolved as of May 6, 2010. Through her lawyer, Suu Kyi asked that "not only the NLD party, but also other ethnic political parties and even families of political prisoners, take up legal proceedings against the election laws." She also said that "the NLD would not be destroyed," even though their offices and meeting places were shut down. Instead, the party would continue its activities and struggles for democracy. In an act designed to reassure their supporters, Aung San Suu Kyi and other NLD leaders chose to leave their flag—a gold peacock on a red field—hanging over their dilapidated national headquarters even as the building was being boarded up.

Political observers commended Aung San Suu Kyi's choice. Many believed that the military's attempt to grant Burmese citizens the opportunity to vote in a so-called "democratic" election was only an effort to ingratiate itself with the rest of the world. But by refusing to register her party, Suu Kyi told the world that the junta's claims of fairness, inclusion, and reconciliation were a charade. UN secretary-general Ban Ki-moon said the international community must respect Suu Kyi's judgment.

As was expected for the November 7, 2010 elections, military-supported candidates and former military officers won a majority of the seats in Parliament. Around the world, the elections were widely declared a fraud. In a press statement, former Secretary of State Hillary Rodham Clinton said, "The United States is deeply disappointed by today's elections in Burma....We will continue our call for respect for human rights, immediate and unconditional release of all political prisoners, including Aung San Suu Kyi, and dialogue toward national reconciliation."

Six days later on November 13, 2010, a small motorcade of official vehicles entered Aung San Suu Kyi's compound. A formal release order was read and within 30 minutes, Aung San Suu Kyi was standing on a raised platform outside of her home as hundreds and then thousands of Burmese rushed toward her in celebration. "There are so many things that we have to talk about," she declared.

Aung San Suu Kyi quickly resumed an active role in her disbanded party's activities. In her first official speech to party members and thousands of citizens she insisted that all of Burma must work toward reconciliation. She said, "We must work together. We Burmese tend to believe in fate, but if we want change we have to do it ourselves." She promised that as long as the Burmese people wanted democracy, she would strive to achieve it.

Aung San Suu Kyi began to meet with government leaders and with foreign officials. She considered that it was maybe time to lift sanctions, explaining that "This is the time that Burma needs help." In March 2011, former military officer and prime minister Thein Sein became president. Aung San Suu Kyi visited Napiydaw and held meetings with the new president and other government officials. Not long after, the government began to meet many of Aung San Suu Kyi's demands. New reforms included freeing political prisoners, loosening censorship laws, permitting peaceful public demonstrations, and allowing the NLD to re-register as

Aung San Suu Kyi attends a parliament session in Naypyidaw on
October 18, 2012.

a political party. Aung San Suu Kyi was immediately elected her
party's leader.

On April 1, 2012 national elections were held to fill several
vacant seats in Parliament. The NLD won 43 of the 45 open seats.
One of those elected was Aung San Suu Kyi, and unlike her 1990
election victory, this time Aung San Suu Kyi was sworn into office.

FROM PRISONER TO POLITICIAN

For more than 15 years, Aung San Suu Kyi lived as a prisoner of conscience, bearing her personal sacrifice with dignity and authority.

Today, she is a Member of Parliament and an international advocate for democracy and human rights. Former secretary of state Clinton recently compared Suu Kyi's experience to that of Nelson Mandela, "They were both marked by uncommon grace, generosity of spirit and unshakable will and they both understood something we all have to grasp. The day they walked out of prison, the day the house arrest was ended, was not the end of the struggle. It was the beginning of a new phase." But some close observers suggest that her future may become as daunting as her past.

Now living in a small concrete home in the capital city of Napyidaw, Aung San Suu Kyi has her long awaited "place at the table." She repeatedly states that she wants reconciliation. To see life improve for her countrymen and women, Suu Kyi insists that she must compromise and negotiate with government officials and the military. Some followers do not like the idea of compromise with a regime that held its citizens in a stranglehold for more than a half century. But Suu Kyi explains that bargaining is "normal and natural now that people are free to talk and argue."

At Suu Kyi's urging, the government is making gestures that suggest reform and democracy. It has allowed trade unions to form and independent newspapers to be published. But thousands of political prisoners remain in jail and ethnic conflict is erupting. To this Aung San Suu Kyi stated, "The high poverty rates in ethnic states clearly indicate that development in ethnic regions is not satisfactory—and ethnic conflicts in these regions have not ceased." Outside of NLD headquarters Suu Kyi declared, "Democracy is when the people keep a government in check. To achieve democracy we need to create a network, not just in our country but around the world. I will try to do that. If you do nothing, you get nothing."

The government knows the world is watching and knows that the key to acceptance by the global community is the voice of Aung San Suu Kyi. After 24 years, she is allowed to travel without concern for prosecution. In her first year of freedom, she visited five countries—Switzerland, where she addressed the International Labor Organization; Ireland; France; England, where she spoke before both houses of Parliament, the only woman besides the Queen who has done so; and Norway, where 21 years after she was honored with the Nobel Peace Prize, she accepted the award to a 30-minute standing ovation. In 2012, Aung San Suu Kyi traveled to the United States to accept the U.S. Congressional Gold Medal.

Looking to the future in a speech at her alma matter, Oxford University, Aung San Suu Kyi said, "Burma is at the beginning of a road. It is not the sort of road that you find in England: it is not smooth; it is not well-maintained; in fact, it is not yet there....This is a road that we will have to build for ourselves, inch by difficult inch....I hope that you will understand that this road is there in our hearts and minds, and that we will need your help and the help of others all around the world to make sure that it leads to where we want our country to go."

When Aung San Suu Kyi was awarded the Nobel Peace Prize in 1991, she was the only person to receive the award while imprisoned. Announcing the award, the Nobel Committee chairman said, "In the good fight for peace and reconciliation, we are dependent on persons who set examples, persons who can symbolize what we are seeking and mobilize the best in us. Aung San Suu Kyi is just such a person. . . . Knowing she is there gives us confidence and faith in the power of good." Twenty-one years later, Aung San Suu Kyi was able to accept the award in person, saying, "Receiving the Nobel Peace Prize means personally extending my concern for

Myanmar's democratic leader Aung San Suu Kyi meets with Japanese Prime Minister Shinzo Abe on April 18, 2013 in Tokyo, Japan.

democracy and human rights beyond national borders. The Nobel Peace Prize opened up a door in my heart. Let us join hands to try to create a peaceful world where we can sleep in security and wake in happiness."

HONORING AUNG SAN SUU KYI

From the earliest days of her struggle for democracy to the present, the world community has recognized and honored Aung San Suu Kyi's ideals, determination, and valor. She has received more than fifty international honors and awards, including the following.

1990

Thorolf Rafto Memorial Human Rights Award
Named after a Norwegian human rights activist, the award promotes intellectual freedom.

Sakharov Freedom of Thought Award
Presented by the European parliament and named after exiled Russian physicist Andrei Sakharov to honor individuals or organizations for their efforts on behalf of human rights, fundamental freedoms, and opposition to oppression and injustice.

1991

Nobel Peace Prize
Named after Alfred Nobel, Norwegian scientist and pacifist, the Nobel Peace Prize was awarded to Suu Kyi for "her nonviolent struggle for democracy and human rights."

1992

International Simón Bolívar Prize
Presented by the United Nations Education, Scientific, and Cultural Organization and named for Simón Bolívar, the Venezuelan who led Latin America to independence from Spain. This prize honors an individual's contributions to the "freedom, independence and dignity of peoples and to the strengthening of a new international economic, social, and cultural order."

1993

Jawaharlal Nehru Award for International Understanding
Presented by the government of India and named after the Indian prime minister to honor people "for their outstanding contribution to the promotion of international understanding, goodwill, and friendship among peoples of the world."

1995

IRC Freedom Award
Presented by the International Rescue Committee to recognize individuals "for their contributions to the cause of refugees and human freedom."

1996

Pearl S. Buck International Woman of the Year Award
Presented by the Pearl S. Buck Foundation and named after
Nobel Prize- and Pulitzer Prize–winner Pearl S. Buck, an
American humanitarian who was raised by missionaries
in China. The award recognizes "a remarkable woman
whose life and work represent compassion, creativity,
commitment to human rights, care for children, and a
positive vision of the world community."

The Companion of the Order of Australia
The highest Australian honor given to a civilian, the order
honors "eminent achievement and merit of the highest
degree in service to Australia or humanity at large." Aung
San Suu Kyi was recognized for her "outstanding leadership
and great personal courage in the struggle to bring
democracy to Burma."

2000

Presidential Medal of Freedom
The highest civilian honor in the United States, created by
President Truman to recognize noble service in times of war
and later, by President Kennedy, to honor service in times of
peace. President Clinton bestowed the honor on Aung San
Suu Kyi because her "unwavering commitment to securing
a free Burma through nonviolent means is an inspiration to
people around the world."

2007

Honorary Citizenship of Canada

Presented by the Canadian parliament, it is Canada's highest civilian award. Aung San Suu Kyi is only the fourth person in the nation's history to receive the award.

2009

Ambassador of Conscience Award

The highest honor presented by Amnesty International, a human rights organization. Amnesty International and the Irish rock band U2 recognized Suu Kyi for her "exceptional leadership in the fight to protect and promote human rights."

2012

U.S. Congressional Gold Medal

Presented by Speaker Nancy Pelosi who said, "Daw Aung San Suu Kyi walks in the footsteps of her beloved father, Aung San, and the giants of history. For her personal sacrifice, for her inner strength, for her love of Burma and its people, and for being an example of strength and courage to the world, today we are proud to honor her with the Congressional Gold Medal—the highest honor Congress can bestow."

TIMELINE

1942	General Aung San and Daw Khin Kyi marry
1945	Aung San Suu Kyi born on June 19
1947	Her father is assassinated July 19
1960	Daw Khin Kyi appointed ambassador to India; Aung San Suu Kyi accompanies her
1964– 1967	Aung San Suu Kyi attends Saint Hugh's College in Oxford, England
1972	Marries Dr. Michael Aris, January
1988	Leaves England in March to care for her ailing mother in Rangoon
1988	General Ne Win steps down as pro-democracy activists protest against Socialists
1988	Aung San Suu Kyi calls for democracy in her first public speech in front of Shwedagon Pagoda in Rangoon
1988	The National League for Democracy (NLD) is formed. Aung San Suu Kyi is appointed general secretary
1989	Placed under house arrest in July
1990	NLD wins landslide election on May 27. Aung San Suu Kyi is elected prime minister. Junta refuses to honor election results
1991	Awarded the Nobel Peace Prize, accepted in absentia by her sons
1995	Aung San Suu Kyi released from house arrest
1999	March 27, Dr. Aris of cancer dies at age 53

2000	Aung San Suu Kyi campaigns for democracy in Mandalay, violating terms of release and is placed under house arrest
2002	Aung San Suu Kyi released from house arrest
2003	Aung San Suu Kyi and supporters are violently attacked in the village of Depayin. Aung San Suu Kyi placed under house arrest
2002	Aung San Suu Kyi released
2007	Aung San Suu Kyi sentenced to another year of house arrest
2008	Junta drafts new constitution; Aung San Suu Kyi and NLD reject
2009	May 4, American John Yettaw swims across Inya Lake to Aung San Suu Kyi's home and refuses to leave
2009	Aung San Suu Kyi is arrested for violating terms of her house arrest and taken to Insein Prison
2009	August 11, Aung San Suu Kyi is sentenced to 18 more months of house arrest
2010	Aung San Suu Kyi and NLD refuse to participate in 2010 elections; NLD and other pro-democracy groups disband
2010	Junta-backed candidates are victors in November elections
2010	Aung San Suu Kyi is freed from house arrest
2011	Thein Sein elected president. Aung San Suu Kyi becomes leader of re-formed NLD
2012– 2013	Aung San Suu Kyi elected to Parliament, travels abroad seeking support for Burmese development

SOURCE NOTES

Boxed quotes unless otherwise noted

CHAPTER 1

p. 7, Aung San Suu Kyi, "My Father," *Freedom from Fear and Other Writings* (London: Penguin Books, 1991).

p. 21, Aung San Suu Kyi, speech, *NGO Forum on Women*, Beijing, August 1995.

CHAPTER 2

p. 29, par. 2, Yeshua Moser-Puangsuwan, "Gandhian Links to the Struggle in Burma," *The Irrawaddy*, April 2007.

p. 31, Edward Klein, "The Lady Triumphs," *Vanity Fair*, October 1995.

CHAPTER 3

p. 38, Justin Wintle, *Perfect Hostage: A Life of Aung San Suu Kyi, Burma's Prisoner of Conscience* (New York: Skyhorse Publishers, 2007).

p. 42, Kyi, *Freedom from Fear and Other Writings*, p. xix.

CHAPTER 4

p. 48, Kyi, *Freedom from Fear and Other Writings*, p. xix.

p. 48, par. 3, Kyi, "Quest for Democracy," *Freedom from Fear and Other Writings*, 177.

p. 49, par. 1, Andrew Clements, *The Voice of Hope: Aung San Suu Kyi Conversations with Alan Clements* (New York: Seven Stories Press, 1997. p. 101).

p. 49, Kyi, "Freedom from Fear," *Freedom from Fear and Other Writings,*

p. 50, Kyi, speech, *Union Day*, Rangoon, February 2000.

CHAPTER 5

p. 57, Kyi, speech, Rangoon, August 26, 1988.

CHAPTER 6

p. 77, Thomas Bell, "Burmese Junta: Aung San Suu Kyi Must Be Beaten Like a Naughty Child," *The Daily Telegraph*, June 2008.

CHAPTER 7

p. 83, Kate McKeown, "Life under Burma's Military Regime," *BBC News*, June 2006.

p. 83, Sandra Burton, "Aung San Suu Kyi: 'This government is not capable of running the economy'," *Time* Asia, November 15, 1999.

p. 85, Jeanne Hallacy, Interview with Aung San Suu Kyi, September 1987.

p. 85, Kyi, commencement address, delivered by Michael Aris, American University, Washington, D.C., January 1997.

p. 86, Ron Gluckman, interview, Aung San Suu Kyi residence, Rangoon, May 1995.

p. 88, Ibid.

p.90, Kyi, statement read by UN envoy Ibrahim Gambari, "Myanmar's Suu Kyi says ready to cooperate with govt," *Reuters*, November 8, 2007.

p. 94, par. 1, Kyi and Alexander Aris, acceptance speech for Nobel Peace Prize, Oslo, Norway, October 14, 1991.

p. 94, Kyi, interview with John Simpson, "Aung San Suu Kyi aims for peaceful revolution," *BBC News Asia Pacific*, November 15, 2010.

FURTHER INFORMATION

BOOKS

Larkin, Emma. *Finding George Orwell in Burma*. New York: Penguin Books, 2006.

Saw, Myar Yin. *Myanmar*. (Cultures of the World). New York: Marshall Cavendish, 2011.

Thomas, Willima. *Aung San Suu Kyi*. Milwaukee, WI: World Almanac Library, 2005.

Wintle, Justin. *Perfect Hostage: A Life of Aung San Suu Kyi, Burma's Prisoner of Conscience*. New York: Skyhorse Publishers, 2007.

WEBSITES

Burma Democratic Concern
www.bdcburma.org/Assk.asp

Burma Net News
Compilations of all news articles published about Burma.
www.burmanet.org/news/

Aung San Suu Kyi's Pages
www.dassk.com/

Democratic Voice of Burma
Radio, Television, and Online Newsmagazine.
Oslo, Norway. 1992–
www.dvb.no/

The Freedom Campaign
Chaired by Bishop Desmond Tutu, sponsored by the Human
Rights Action Center and the U.S. Campaign for Burma.
www.thefreedomcampaign.org/

The Irrawaddy e
Online version. Bangkok: Irrawaddy Publishing Group. 1992-
www.irrawaddy.org/

U.S. Campaign for Burma
http://uscampaignforburma.org/

DVDS

Boorman, John, with Patricia Arquette, U Aung Ko, Frances
McDormand, and Spalding Gray. *Beyond Rangoon*. Warner
Home Video, 1995.

Østergaard, Anders. *Burma VJ: Reporting from a Closed Country*.
Oscilloscope Laboratories, 2009.

BIBLIOGRAPHY

BOOKS

Abrams, Irwin. *The Nobel Peace Prize*. New York: Seven Stories Press, 1993.

Aung San Suu Kyi, Aung San Suu. *Freedom from Fear and Other Writings*. London: Penguin Books, 1991.

Aung San Suu Kyi, Aung San Suu. *The Voice of Hope*. New York: Seven Stories Press, 1997.

Clements, Alan, with Aung San Suu Kyi. *The Voice of Hope: Conversations with Aung San Suu Kyi*. New York: Seven Stories Press, 1997.

Marshall, Andrew. *The Trouser People: A Story of Burma in the Shadow of the Empire*. Berkeley, CA: Counterpoint Press, 2001.

Thomas, Willima. *Aung San Suu Kyi*. Milwaukee, WI: World Almanac Library, 2005.

Victor, Barbara. *The Lady: Aung San Suu Kyi, Nobel Laureate and Burma's Prisoner*. Boston: Faber & Faber, 1998.

Wintle, Justin. *Perfect Hostage: A Life of Aung San Suu Kyi, Burma's Prisoner of Conscience*. New York: Skyhorse Publishers, 2007.

WEBSITES

"Asia Pacific: Burma." *BBC News World*. http://news.bbc.co.uk/

Burma Democratic Concern. www.bdcburma.org/Assk.asp

Burma Net News. www.burmanet.org/news/

Campaign for Burma, United Kingdom. Aung San Suu Kyi Biography. www.burmacampaign.org.uk

CIA World Fact Book. Burma. www.cia.gov/library/publications/ the-world-factbook/geos/bm.html

Daw Aung San Suu Kyi's Pages. www.dassk.com/

Democratic Voice of Burma. www.dvb.no/

*Freedom Campaign.*www.thefreedomcampaign.org/

The Guardian. Manchester, UK: Guardian News and Media Limited. www.guardian.co.uk/

The Irrawaddy Newsmagazine, Burma, Myanmar and Southeast Asia. www.irrawaddy.org

National Coalition Government of the Union of Burma. www.ncgub.net

"Times Topics—Myanmar." *New York Times.* www.nytimes.com/ info/myanmar/

Time World Edition. www.time.com/time/world

ARTICLES

"Aung San Suu Kyi," *Newsmakers*, Issue 2, Farmington Hills, MI: Gale, 2009.

Barron, Meghan and Jared Genser, "The Burmese Junta Still Fears Suu Kyi." *Wall Street Journal.* Vol. CCLIII, No. 115, May 18, 2009.

Bell, Thomas, "Burmese Junta: Aung San Suu Kyi Must Be Beaten Like a Naughty Child," *The Daily Telegraph*, June 2008. www.telegraph.co.uk/news/worldnews/asia/burmamyanmar/2110450/Burmese-junta-compares-repression-to-UK-anti-terror-laws.html

Bureau of East Asian and Pacific Affairs, "Burma: U.S. Department of State Background Notes," January 31, 2010.

Gluckman, Ron, "The Lady and the Tramps," *Aung San Suu Kyi Talks*, 1995. www.gluckman.com/AungSanSuuKyi.html

Harris, Bruce, "Daw Aung San Suu Kyi," *Heroes and Killers of the 20th Century*, January 2009. www.moreorless.au.com/heroes/suukyi.html

Kaplan, Robert, "Lifting the Bamboo Curtain," *The Atlantic*, September 2008, pp. 84–95.

Kristof, Nicholas, "Sneaking In Where Thugs Rule," *New York Times*, February 4, 2009.

Marshall, Andrew, "Burma: Justice for All," *Time World Edition*, August 24, 2009. www.time.com/time/magazine/article/0,9171,1916096,00.html

Nobel Peace Prize 1991. Proc. of Nobel Peace Prize, Oslo, Norway. Norwegian Nobel Committee, 1991, http://nobelprize.org/nobel_prizes/peace/laureates/1991/

Vaknin, Sam, "The Aung San Family in Myanmar," *Global Politician Magazine*, September 2005. http://globalpolitician.com/21178-myanmar-burma

INDEX

independence movements
  Burmese independence, 8, 10-11, 12-13,
    15-16, 18
  ethnic groups and, 26, 27, 28
international aid, Cyclone Nargis and, 76, 77
international relations, 20, 77, 78, 79, 83, 90
  2010 elections and, 81, 85, 86, 90
  economic sanctions and, 84, 85, 86, 91
  Yettaw incident and, 80-81
Islam, 27-28

Japan, 12-13, **14**, 15-16, 43-45

Kachin people, 27
Karenni people, 28
Karen people, **25**, 25-26
Khin Kyi, 13-14, 15, **20**, **32**, 44
  death of, 62-63
  marriage of Aung San Suu Kyi and, 42, 43
  public service and, 19-21, 34-35, 36
  World War II and, 18-19, 33-34

mail and visits, during house arrest, 67, 71
Ma Than E, 38, 40
military government, 49-50, 78-79
Democracy Summer and, 56-57, 58-59
  economic policies of, 87-90
  election laws and, 83-84, 85
  ethnic groups and, 29, 31, 55
  National League for Democracy (NLD) and,
    62-65
Mon people, 28
Myanmar. *See* Burma

naming customs, 33
National League for Democracy (NLD),
  62-65, 68, 69, 72-75, 76-77, 87, 88-93
National Union Party, 19
National Unity Party (NUP), 59, 62
natural disasters, 76-77
natural resources, 23-24, 55
Naypyidaw (Burmese capital), 78
Nehru, Jawaharlal, 12, 36, 56
Ne Win, 31, 43, **54**, 56, 59
news media, 71
Nobel Peace Prize, 94-96, 98
nonviolence, 73, 95

Panglong Agreement, 16
personal life
  childhood of, **20**, 34-36
    employment, 40-41

during house arrest, 69-71
marriage and, 41-43
separation from family and, 65, 73-74
university education and, 37-38, 40,
  43-45
public symbol, Aung San Suu Kyi as, 92-95

religious beliefs
  Buddhism, 18, 25, 47-48, 70-71
  Christian missionaries and, 25, 27, 29, 51
  ethnic groups and, 25, 26, 27, 29
  Islam, 27-28
  Michael Aris and, 39-40

Saw Maung, 59, 62
Shan people, 26
Shwegondaing Declaration, 85
speeches, 56, 57-58, **59**, 60-61, 72
standard of living, Burmese, 83, 84, 85
State Law and Order Restoration Council
  (SLORC), 58, 62-63, 64-65, 68, 72, 73-74
  See also military government
State Peace and Development Council
  (SPDC), 74
states and regions, of Burma, 24

"Ten Duties of Kings," 47-48
Thangyat chants, 52-53
Than Shwe, 65, 78, 80, 85
Thant, U, 40
Thingyan Festival, 52, 53
Thirty Comrades, Burmese independence
  movement and, 12-13
Timeline, 100-101
trade, economic policies and, 84, 85, 86, 91
travel
  within Burma, 74, 75
  obtaining visas and, 62, 73-74, 76, 81
trials, Aung San Suu Kyi and, 67, 68, 80-81

Union Solidarity and Development
  Association (USDA), 75
United Nations, 38, 40-41, 42, 49
United Wa State Army, 27
Universal Declaration of Human Rights, 49

Wa people, 26-27
Women's Freedom League, 13-14
World War II, 12-13, 13-15, **14**, 25-26

Year of the Revolution, 10-11
Yettaw, John, 80, 81